To Benji
Best wishes
to a Rice Man —

You Better Be Right!

My 25 Years as an SEC Football Official

Dick Burleson

ISBN: 0-9768147-0-6

Printed in the United States of America
EBSCO Media
Birmingham, Alabama

Dedication

I dedicate this book to all past and present SEC football officials, coaches, players, and fans of college football— the greatest game ever.

Contents

Foreword

This is a book that needed to be written. There have been numerous books written by officials about their experiences in the National Football League. This, however, is the first book written by a college official about the challenges of officiating in the SEC (Southeastern Conference), a conference many consider to be the most competitive and athletic in all of college football and with fans considered to be the most passionate in America. No one is better qualified to tell the story than Dick Burleson, who over the course of 25 years became one of the conference's best and most respected officials.

It was a privilege to observe Dick Burleson in action. His schedule was such that he worked more Georgia games than any other conference school while I was coaching. I always was impressed by the professional manner in which he handled his duties.

Officials like Dick Burleson have an awesome responsibility. They not only must thoroughly know the rules of the game, they are also charged with making split-second decisions that affect the outcome of a game—and possibly the fate of a football coach.

Being an official in the SEC—where football borders on being a religion—requires personal commitment, dedication, and love for the game. Dick is a classic example.

Dick's background prepared him for making tough decisions. He is vice president of one of the largest engineering firms in the United States, served in the Army Reserve, and rose to the rank of major general. He served as commanding general of the 81st Regional Support Command, the largest armed forces reserve command in the world, which covered eight states and 40,000 troops. Five thousand of those troops were active in Desert

Storm, and General Colin Powell personally congratulated General Burleson's units in 1995. General Burleson's highest personal honor came when he received the Spirit of America's Audie Murphy Patriotism Award. The SEC also honored General Burleson by selecting him to be chief referee and president of the conference's officials and to officiate numerous major bowl games. His last honor came when he was selected to be head referee for the 1998 National Championship game at the Rose Bowl.

Dick's book covers the many challenges he faced while coming up through the ranks as an inexperienced high-school official before finally being accepted into the SEC. Though Dick was an excellent athlete, he did not play SEC football. Few, if any, are welcomed into the SEC as an official who have not played SEC football, but Dick's expertise was evident from his first game.

Dick's book chronicles some of the great rivalries in the conference as well as some of the great coaches who roamed SEC sidelines. He takes his readers inside an official's game-day experience, explaining the duties of each official and how correct positioning allows each man to be in the right position to make the correct call. Dick also reviews some of the SEC's greatest players and some of the experiences, many humorous, that took place during the course of the game—sometimes at the most serious moments.

I salute Dick Burleson for providing fans, coaches, and players with a real insight into how officials operate in the SEC. His book will certainly bring a new respect for the men in stripes.

Well done, General Burleson.

Coach Vince Dooley, University of Georgia

Preface

To my knowledge, no SEC official has ever written a book about officiating. SEC officials are successful businessmen who love the game but make mistakes like anyone else. We are actually held to a higher standard than players or coaches, which we readily accept, but no one hurts over a missed call more than the official who made it.

So why do we do it? Well, I try to explain in this book. Although I include many humorous incidents from my 25-year career as an SEC official, officiating SEC football is serious business. Every SEC official tries to make perfect calls to ensure the integrity of the game. Our axiom is "Don't call everything you see—but see everything you call."

I thought about making that principle the title of this book, but I chose instead something Coach Bear Bryant said to me during the 1982 Alabama-Vanderbilt game: "You better be right!"

A Vandy linebacker sacks the Alabama quarterback 10 yards behind the line of scrimmage, but in doing so, grabs his face mask. It is a 15-yard penalty, but at this time it is assessed from the spot of the foul, which is behind the line of scrimmage instead of from the line of scrimmage itself, as is done nowadays. Alabama only ends up gaining about 5 yards or so.

Coach Bryant doesn't understand why the penalty is assessed that way, and I don't know if he ever really understood it, but I know for a fact that it is the right call. Nevertheless, he is not happy with it. He is never one to rant and rave and make a fool of himself, but a little while later, one of my side officials comes up to me and tells me the coach wants to see me during the next timeout.

The ball changes hands, and time is called to allow the radio stations a break. I ease over to the Alabama sideline to see what he has on his mind. He looks perplexed. "Tell me about that penalty we had there," he says.

I explain why he gained only 5 yards on a 15-yard penalty.

"Are you sure about that?" he asks.

"Yes, Sir."

"Ok." He turns around to walk away, and I begin to walk back to midfield. "Hey, Dick," he says.

I turn around. "Yes, Sir?"

"You better be right!" he says.

I hope you enjoy reading this book as much as I enjoyed writing it.

Acknowledgments

I owe much to a lot of individuals in my life and to those who influenced my officiating career. In addition, several people were instrumental in helping me write this book. A thank you to some special people:

To my parents, Joe and Lucille Burleson;

To my grandparents Henry and Nan Ratliff, my role model;

To my high-school teachers and principal, Mr. Pennington;

To my coaches, Coach Starkey and Coach Driskell;

To high-school leaders including Cliff Harper, Bubba Scott, and Dan Washburn;

To Jim Lester, who was my greatest officiating supporter;

To former leaders of SEC officiating who set officiating standards including George Gardner, Gordon Pettus, Pete Williams, and George Morris;

To all the soldiers I was privileged to serve with;

To great employees at CBI, CTE, DMJM-Harris, and AECOM;

To Paul Finebaum for his encouragement to write this book;

To Trey McClure for his writing talent;

To Judy Clark, Bob Weathers, and Norma McKittrick for publishing support;

To all my wonderful family and close friends;

To nephew Justin McBurney for showing all of us what courage is all about;

To niece Stephanie and nephew Jake Gossett who
   showed us what grandparenting is about;

To my children, Richard and Mary Jo, whom I love
   dearly and have always made me proud;

To our grandson, Richie, who is a special, wonderful
   blessing in our life;

And to Mary, my life's love and greatest supporter.

Introduction

I was born on June 16, 1939, in my father's hometown of Hartselle, Alabama, and I grew up in Blountsville, a small town about halfway between Birmingham and Huntsville. Since my father was an officer in the Army, I was raised by my grandparents, Henry and Nancy "Nan" Ratliff. I've been asked many times over the years about my childhood role model. I always answer my grandmother. She was my greatest supporter—whether I was right or wrong, she gave me total support and innate strength.

While most boys had a favorite player they looked up to, Andy Griffith sparked my love of football. Before he became a TV sheriff, he was an accomplished comedian. The B&R Café, a local hangout in Blountsville, had one of his records on the jukebox. On it was a classic segment called "What It Was, Was Football." You may have heard it before; if not, I suggest you give it a listen. It's as funny today as it was then. In it, he describes a football game from the point of view of a complete stranger, going into the details of "the awfulest fight I ever did see." He repeatedly refers to a group of "convicts" that break up the fighting every few seconds. Little did I know at the time that I would grow up to become one of those convicts.

I attended J.B. Pennington High School in Blountsville from 1953 to 1957. Like most boys in the '50s, I liked all sports, but I concentrated on basketball and football, which was a great experience. My years at Pennington instilled in me a set of morals and values that shaped the person I would become. I would be remiss if I neglected to mention the teachers and coaches who taught me lessons in and out of the classroom, teachers like Ms. Porter, Ms. Shepard, and Ms. Cox, and coaches like Coach Starkey and Coach Driskell, who doubled as father figures for me when I sorely needed them. And then there was the namesake of the school, J.B. Pennington himself, who was principal of the school during my tenure. He was a man of impeccable character who expected no less from his faculty and students.

That's exactly what he got. The school was spotless, free from the vandalism and graffiti that can result from the destructive nature of teenagers. The lockers had no locks, as decreed by Mr. Pennington, but this was not a problem. In my four years there, only once did an item turn up missing. Mr. Pennington called an assembly to announce that a girl's shoes had apparently been placed in the wrong locker and he expected them to be back in their proper place by the end of the day. They were.

I have found through talking with other officials that most people who put on the striped shirt can point to a specific person who steered them down that path or at least planted the idea in their head. Rarely do you find someone whose lifelong dream was to become a football official—it's generally suggested by someone else. For me, that someone else was a teacher at Pennington, a man named Mr. Pribbenow. He was one of my favorite teachers, and in addition to that, he was a tremendously successful high-school basketball official. We forged a friendship through classes and basketball. Every year before the season started, he would take me into the gym by myself and explain to me the new rules for that year. Not only would he show them to me, but he would also give me tips on how to use them to my advantage. Needless to say, he was a great help to my high-school basketball career.

In spite of my friendship with Mr. Pribbenow, I still knew very little about officials. I was like most kids playing high-school ball—I didn't know who they were, where they came from, or anything else about them. All I knew was that when I played games, these men in striped shirts showed up, we yelled at them for ruining our games, and they went home. We never gave it much thought. What else did we need to know?

Before moving on, I have to mention one last thing, which I consider the most important. Of all the things J.B. Pennington High School meant to me, the most important is that I met the love of my life, Mary, there when she was 13 and I was 14. We have been together ever since.

Going to Georgia Tech and Getting My First Taste of Officiating

I graduated from Pennington in 1957 with my heart set on an engineering degree. For my money, the best engineering school in the country was the Georgia Institute of Technology. Even in high school I had a love for Georgia Tech. Its academic and athletic reputation impressed me, and I turned down other scholarships to go there. My love for Tech is still as strong today, and I consider the combination of academics and athletics to be unsurpassed anywhere. I began my studies that fall, majoring in civil engineering.

My interest in officiating was rekindled during my time at Tech. My roommate had an uncle who was a high-school football official. One Friday night when we had nothing to do, his uncle invited us to carry the chains at a local game. It sounded like more fun than sitting around the dorm room or hanging out at The Varsity, so we agreed to do it.

This was my first taste of what officiating was all about. Now I had been on the field hundreds of times; I knew what the game felt like from a player's point of view. Never had I seen it from this perspective. Riding in the car on the way to the game, I began to see the personalities behind the "convict" shirts. I saw that these men had a genuine love for the game; they did what they did just to be close to the action. I could sense the camaraderie and genuine friendship between them—this was a sort of fraternity of striped-shirt individuals sharing something they all truly loved. This made quite an impression on a 19-year-old; I realized this was something I wanted to do.

Officiating My First Game

I graduated from Georgia Tech in the summer of 1961 with a degree in Civil Engineering, was commissioned as an Army Lieutenant, wed Mary, and immediately shipped out to Fort Belvoir, Virginia, to begin two years of service in the Army. During my time there and at Fort Leonard Wood in Missouri, I was looking for something to fill the sports void in my life. I was approached by the post Special Services Officer who said he had heard I had an athletic background and asked if I had any interest in helping them officiate basketball games on and off-post. I said I did, and within a week I was officiating a basketball game on the base. And thus my career as an official began, working basketball games on Fort Leonard Wood in 1962.

Surprising as it may seem, my first sports love was basketball. I had no real intention of officiating football at first, but the understanding on the base was that all basketball officials had to double as football officials and vice versa. So by default my football officiating career began there as well.

Two years later I finished my active duty, left Fort Leonard Wood, and began work for a firm called Chicago Bridge and Iron Co. (CB&I), an outstanding company with great people in Birmingham, Alabama. I would end up working there for 30 years. My interest in officiating was at a peak at that time, so I wanted to get into it as soon as possible.

Officiating High-School Football Games

I came to find out that there was a state officiating board, the Alabama High School Athletic Association (AHSAA), that I had to join. Membership in the AHSAA came through local officials associations, which were located in most cities and towns of significant size. There were two in Birmingham, one of which was the oldest and largest chapter in the state, the Birmingham Football Officials Association (BFOA). The head of that group was a man named Dan Gaylord, who was an icon in officiating. Everybody knew Mr. Gaylord. He ran a service station in Woodlawn, so if you wanted to see him, that's where you went. I went to his service station, and he sat me down in his office and had me take my first Alabama High School Official's Exam. We became good friends, and I spent a total of 15 years as a member of the BFOA.

To this day I contend that the BFOA is one of the finest high-school organizations anywhere. The group has supplied the college ranks with a multitude of great officials over the years, and it continues to do so today. The group also has provided me with some of my very best and closest friends.

Mr. Gaylord knew that I came in with experience, and that counted for something. On my application I had to list which positions I preferred. I, of course, said that I wanted to be a head referee since that's what I'd always been. My second choice was head linesman.

On the way to officiate my first high-school football game, riding in the car with three other officials all of whom have years of experience, I remember sitting quietly in the back, nervous about my first game, while they crack jokes and generally have a good time. As we get closer to the game, they take a vote to see who will be the head referee for the game. Being the new guy, I abstain.

At first I think it's a joke when they vote me head ref. I figure it's just a ploy to scare me, and a successful one at that. I keep waiting for them to relent and decide who will actually do the job. They never do. We arrive at the stadium and walk out on the field, and it becomes evident that I am actually going to be the head referee. My first-ever high-school game will also be my first experience as head referee. I try to remain confident—how hard could it be? I know the rules, the signals, the procedures—I should be ready.

Just five years after I last removed my pads and helmet, I take the field as head referee. The game gets under way, and things run surprisingly smoothly. As the quarters progress, I gain more and more confidence. I'm getting the hang of it; refereeing is easier than I thought. The game is close, but I'm on top of it. Nothing comes along that I can't handle—everything is under control.

Somewhere in the middle of the fourth quarter though, I get my first real test. The game is neck-and-neck, and the home team has the ball on the visiting team's 45-yard line. The play is supposed to be a swing pass to the fullback somewhere near the line of scrimmage. Everything works basically as planned—the quarterback drops back and tosses the ball over to the fullback, but the play develops a bit more quickly than the fullback had planned, and he isn't ready for the pass. The ball hits him in the chest and bounces off. End of play. The problem is that the fullback is a bit slow and doesn't quite make it in front of the quarterback, so instead of an incomplete pass, it's actually a backward pass—the ball is still live. I am apparently the only person in the stadium who notices this. There is no signal for "backward pass" at the time—the only way to tell is that I don't whistle the play dead. The fullback walks off, leaving the ball lying there. Everybody starts to regroup for the next play, and I'm just standing there, with the ball a few yards away, not sure what to do.

Just when I'm about to give up and spot the ball for the next play, I see a defensive end standing there looking at me. He seems confused; he can tell something is up, but he's not sure what. He looks at the ball, then back at me, as if to ask what the deal is. Bad as I want to tell him it's a live ball, in the interest of fairness I keep my mouth shut. He takes a few tentative steps toward me, looks up, and a big grin crosses his face as he realizes the ball is his for the taking. I try to remain neutral, but I can't help but let a bit of a smile creep out. He takes this as his signal that everything is all right, walks over, and picks up the ball. Still nobody else on the field notices. He looks at me and nods, and I nod back at him. He begins to slowly walk toward the goal line, and I walk with him, following the ball. Even now, nobody notices what is happening, and he walks untouched into the end zone for what would end up being the winning touchdown.

Looking back, I can't think of a more fitting way for my officiating career to have begun. This type of incident would prove to be the rule rather than the exception throughout my career.

Before I go any further, I need to mention a couple of people I credit for furthering my career. One was Cliff Harper, who was head of the AHSAA at the time. A man of great integrity, he was very popular among his peers because he demanded and got the best out of everyone involved. He was instrumental not only in my development as a high-school official but also as a college official since he moved up to the Southeastern Conference as a supervisor of officials about the same time as I went there as a referee.

Another official I met through BFOA who would become a good friend was Jim Lester. We worked a lot of football games together, he as an umpire and I as head referee. He was very helpful in getting my career in college officiating started. When the original Gulf South Conference was formed in 1968, he was hired as the first supervisor of the conference's officials. He chose me as one of the charter members of their officiating group, and to this day I thank him for taking a chance on me.

Moving Up to College Football Officiating

I left the BFOA a few years later to devote my time solely to college football. I have nothing but good memories of that organization, and the feeling is mutual. One of the greatest honors I have ever received was when they named their annual award for outstanding officiating after me.

You may wonder what happened to my basketball officiating career. As I said, basketball was my first love, but football is where I ended up making my name. As it turns out, it was a matter of logistics. When I got home from active military duty in 1963, I began working high-school games, both football and basketball. Football was simple, one night a week, short season, nothing to it. Basketball, on the other hand, was extremely time-consuming. Basketball officials were expected to work almost every night at high-school, church-league, and junior-high games—anywhere they needed officials, you were expected to go. Plus the season is a couple of months longer, so it takes up even more of your time. In 1966 my son, Richard, was born. By 1968 I had been working both sports for about five years as well as serving in the Army Reserve.

I came home one night from a long session of basketball, and my wife, Mary, sat me down to talk. "Look," she told me, "I know you love to officiate, and I love for you to do it, but we have a new child, and we both need you around more. Between football, basketball, the Reserve, and your job, you're stretched thin. I wish you would at least focus on a single sport so you can give more time to us." I knew one sport would have to go, and frankly football took less of my time. That would be the last season I would officiate basketball.

I think one of the great honors one receives as a football official is simply the chance to work with the coaches and players on Friday nights. I consider high-school football the epitome of all that is good in scholastic activities. This is not to demean other sports, but football is a rallying point for a whole community, and it is a great thrill to work a game, not to mention the most fun anyone can have. It's a serious thing, of course, as is all officiating, but working with high-school kids and coaches is a wonderful experience. I met a lot of great coaches working high-school games, and I couldn't name them all if I wanted to, but there were a couple who really stood out.

One is Bill Legg, who was director of Jefferson County athletics at the time and has since gone on to head the Alabama Sports Hall of Fame. He was a tremendous coach and administrator and did an amazing job of making sure things were done properly in Jefferson County.

I couldn't say this until after I retired from high-school officiating, but my favorite high-school coach of all time was Bob Finley, who was coach of Berry High School for many years, and the finest coach, finest teacher, and finest person I have ever had the privilege to work with. This isn't to say he didn't get upset at bad calls like everyone else, but he understood that once the game was over, that was that. No matter what happened during the game, on the way off the field he would shake your hand and thank you for a job well done whether he felt it or not. That was his style—it was what he taught his players and assistants, and it was what he truly believed. There were a lot like him, but Bob Finley epitomized what high-school athletics should be all about.

There are thousands of high-school officials across the Southeast, most of whom would love to work in college, especially the SEC. The majority of them don't get the chance because they just never get a break. I was fortunate to be chosen as an official for the Gulf South Conference, and I spent four good years there.

When I joined the Southeastern Conference (SEC) in 1972, I was only the second person to my knowledge to start out in the SEC as a head referee, the other being Jimmy Harper. I was also one of the youngest officials in the conference at 32 years old. Joining the conference at that age was unusual at that time, as it is today. When I got to be part of the selection process, I learned exactly how fortunate I was to be selected at that age.

Chapter 1

The Life of a Football Official

Football officiating is not a full-time job, which is a popular misconception among football fans and observers. It is a hobby, a paid hobby—but a hobby nonetheless. I like to refer to officiating as an avocation.

Football officials come from all walks of life, an interesting cross-section of society united by a shared love for the game. Most officials have experience playing the game on some level for part of their lives; very few make it without having some on-field experience. One thing all officials share is a burning love for the game, a need to stay involved in football in some way while maintaining an outside life.

I was no exception. As soon as I graduated from Georgia Tech, I had to find a way to remain close to the action. I knew I didn't want to coach; I went to school for engineering, and that's how I wanted to make my living. I couldn't stay away from the game though, so I turned to officiating.

To answer a couple of other questions I am frequently asked on radio shows and at speaking engagements: Yes, you have to be a member of some organization to officiate games. No, there aren't specific classes you have to take to learn how to be an official. There are no freelance officials. To work games at any level, you must belong to an organization that governs officials. To get into these organizations, you have to pass a test to show that you know the rules. Though some places have classes in football officiating, these are not required by any group. Each conference has its own rules test, and it doesn't matter how you acquired that knowledge.

Basically the way it works is that when you sign up with an officiating organization, you go through an evaluation process. You begin by taking a test to see if you know the rules, terminology, signals, and so on. If you pass the test, you start out working little-league games, middle-school games, junior varsity high-school games, etc. If you show you have an aptitude for officiating, they give you a chance at high-school varsity. The exact protocol varies by league and region, but that's essentially how it works. When you're finally accepted, you have to go through more training to keep yourself physically and mentally fit for the job.

Becoming an SEC Football Official

When I joined in 1972, the selection process in the Southeastern Conference (SEC) was governed by a committee of three active coaches and three active officials, with a supervisor of officials acting as the tiebreaker. Every year they would search through a few hundred applications, weed out the unqualified ones, and pick from the rest. To be considered, an official had to have a decent amount of experience and at least two other officials and at least one active coach to speak on his behalf.

One man I thank for helping me get my foot in the SEC door was Gordon Pettus, an established official in the conference who was instrumental in my selection. We were friends from our days working high-school games, and he put in a good word for me when my name came up. He would later go on to become the supervisor of officials for the conference.

When I started, a person could join the SEC straight from working high-school games with no college experience. They would gain this experience by working freshman SEC games or smaller schools like Sewanee for a couple of years. Generally they would start out as clock operator and work their way onto the field over time.

The process is different today. Scholarship limitations have eliminated freshman games, and so the standards for entry into the conference are tougher. We don't even consider an official unless he has worked successfully in small-college football for a few seasons. Also, coaches no longer have any input into the selection of officials. There is a group of technical advisors (of which I am a member) who meet every January with a supervisor to pick the new officials. The applications come to us prescreened, with the unqualified individuals weeded out. This quickens the process considerably. We keep a roster of around 70 officials, and retirements and promotions to the National Football League usually give us about two openings per year.

Our daughter, Mary Jo, was born on September 27, 1972. I had been assigned to officiate my first SEC freshman game, Tennessee versus Vanderbilt, scheduled to be played just three days later. To this day I thank Mary Jo for going ahead and coming into the world in time for me to make that game.

Somewhere during my second year in the conference, I was assigned a real SEC varsity game, Vanderbilt versus the University of Tampa. This was far and away the highest profile game I had ever officiated. Even though the game meant very little, to me it was the most important game of the season. Considering my history, I really expected something bizarre or noteworthy to happen during that game, but everything went smoothly. It was an easy game, and in that inauspicious manner, my SEC career began in earnest.

Meetings and Crews

In the Southeastern Conference, there are mandatory meetings twice a year, a mini-clinic during the spring and a mandatory meeting in August. These are to make sure everybody is up to date on the new rules and in good enough physical shape to make it through a whole season. If somebody shows up out of shape in the spring, they have until the next meeting to shape up or they're not allowed to officiate that season. There is also a 1½-mile run during the August meeting, which has to be accomplished in a certain time. There are mechanics and rules tests as well to make sure everybody still remembers all the rules and regulations.

The second meeting is also important because that's where we explain the new rules and their interpretations to the head and assistant coaches. We also show them what existing rules the NCAA (National Collegiate Athletic Association) is emphasizing for that season (if they want us to focus on roughing the passer, holding, pass interference, etc.).

Another service we provide is supplying officials for scrimmages and practices. Some schools request full officiating crews at all their practices, but every school at least wants them at their scrimmages and spring games. This works to everybody's advantage—we get practice enforcing new rules, and the coaches get to see exactly how the new rules work. We also visit each school and conduct a rules clinic for the coaching staff and players, just to make sure everybody is together on everything. This usually happens somewhere around the second week of fall practice. We go more in depth at this time, showing new interpretations of rules and what new twists we will be calling that we hadn't before.

In the SEC, we work in crews. This means that the same group works together for the whole season, in the same positions, except where there are conflicts of interest. This is a fairly recent development, and not one with which I initially agreed.

The reasoning behind the crew system is that younger officials get to learn by working with older, more experienced officials. The way it worked prior to the institution of the crew system was that young officials worked their way up, starting with freshman games and moving up to SEC games of lesser importance, while the big games were worked by more experienced officials. Today, you may have a third-year linesman or back judge working with a referee and umpire who has been in the business for 20 years. The idea behind the crew system is that all SEC games are of equal importance.

We used to use split crews for intersectional games, such as when an SEC team and a Big 10 team played each other, half of the officiating crew would be SEC and half would be Big 10. That doesn't happen anymore. These days, whichever team is on the road generally furnishes its own crew. This is done mainly to even things out and eliminate the perception of home favoritism, at least in the minds of the visiting team and their fans. Unlike the use of solid crews, this is not a stipulation of the NCAA rulebook; rather it is something agreed upon when the teams sign the contract for the game.

Coach Joe Paterno of Penn State told me that he and Coach Paul Bryant of Alabama started this practice. As he tells it, during a game up in State College, Pennsylvania, an official that Penn State had provided made a call that caused quite an uproar, and some people still haven't forgotten about it. They decided from then on that they would only use solid crews during their games, and this became standard practice across the nation. It has since become an NCAA rule.

In bowl assignments, they only use officials from neutral conferences. If an ACC (Atlantic Coast Conference) team is playing a PAC-10 (Pacific Ten Conference) team, the officiating crew has to be from a different conference. This was why I was able to officiate the Rose Bowl as my last game.

Officiating Positions and Duties

During speaking engagements and radio appearances, I'm frequently asked about official positions. What do the letters on officials' backs mean? What do they do? The NCAA rulebook states that a crew of anywhere from four to seven officials may work a game, but you will never see a major conference game officiated by fewer than seven, barring injury. Each official has an individual position with duties unique to that position. Under the crew system we have in place in the SEC, an official works his position all season no matter what game he's working. The seven positions are broken down as follows.

Field Judge: The main duty of the field judge is to observe downfield passes in his area, watching for illegal activity around the ball. He also rules whether passes are complete or not, counts defensive players, and helps return the ball to the line of scrimmage. He lines up approximately 20 yards deep in the defensive backfield, on the sideline, on the press box side of the field.

Side Judge: The side judge is similar to the field judge. He lines up on the opposite sideline from the field judge, about 20 yards into the defensive backfield. His responsibilities are the same as the field judge, with the addition of keeping track of the 25-second clock. Also, on short third and fourth downs and field goals, he moves up and acts as a "double" umpire.

Back Judge: The back judge does essentially the same job as the field and side judges but from the middle of the field and about 5 yards deeper. He watches for illegal men downfield, pass interference, and any other things that may enter his area of the field.

Linesman: The linesman (also sometimes referred to as "head linesman") is responsible for the down and distance indicators. He oversees a crew of three assistants who run the chains and the down indicator. He lines up on the opposite side of the field from the press box, even with the line of scrimmage. His main jobs are to watch for neutral-zone infractions before the play and mark forward progress, as well as to watch the legality of play around the ball when it is in his area.

Line Judge: The line judge essentially duplicates what the linesman does. He stands on the press box side of the field, watching for neutral-zone infractions and illegal offensive formations. He is also responsible for observing the legality of play when the ball comes into his area.

Umpire: The umpire is essentially the same as the referee, just on the opposite side of the line of scrimmage. They work together counting offensive players, keeping track of downs, and working on penalties. When a penalty is assessed, the referee announces it while the umpire steps it off. He sets up 5-7 yards deep in the defensive backfield, where he watches for illegal line play, illegal men downfield, illegal snaps, and whether passes or kicks cross the neutral zone. On kickoffs, he stays with the kicker, watching for infractions from that vantage point. It is also the umpire's duty to make sure all player equipment meets the specifications mandated by the NCAA and/or the conference.

Referee: The referee is the head of the officiating crew, which is why I sometimes refer to the position as "head referee." His decision on penalties is final. His main unique duty is to act as the liaison between the field and the sidelines, press box, and crowd. He is responsible for reporting penalties to the press box and the crowd, signaling down and distance, spotting the ball, and instructing the clock operators when to start and stop the game and play clocks. His other duties include keeping track of downs and time-outs and counting offensive players. The referee's position is behind and to the side of the offensive backfield, where he watches for illegal shifts, illegal blocks, or roughing of the quarterback, kicker, or punter. On kickoffs, the referee takes a position in the end zone with the deep receivers.

For televised games, we add another official to the group: the **Television Liaison**. He dresses in a normal official uniform except with a white shirt and a red hat. He wears a headset so he can talk to the producer of the broadcast and let the head referee know when a TV time-out is requested. He signals the referee when the producer asks for a timeout, but it is up to the referee when and if he grants the request. The broadcasters are entitled to a certain number of timeouts during a game, but when the timeouts occur is up to the head referee. It is also the responsibility of the liaison to let the head referee know when to start getting the players ready to go back on the air. The liaison gives a "30 seconds to go" signal, and the referee gets things going, so that hopefully when they return from commercial, the next play starts immediately thereafter. When they come back in the middle or after a play, something went wrong.

One thing the Southeastern Conference does differently from most other conferences is that we bring our own **Alternate Official (Clock Operator)** to games. Most places let the schools provide them, but we furnish them ourselves. We have an official on the sideline in full uniform with a tethered box running the scoreboard clock. This takes away a little bit of the perceived home-field advantage, in an attempt to make things as neutral as possible. He is used for several purposes apart from running the clock, but his main alternate function is to act as a spare in case one official gets hurt. This was unique to the SEC for a while, but more conferences are picking up on the idea and following suit.

"See everything you call, but don't call everything you see" was going to be the title of this book, but was a bit too long. It would have been a good one since it sums up the philosophy most officials follow. Another axiom is to make sure it is a "quality foul." Basically it means be selective in the flags you throw, and make sure you can back them up. There's nothing worse than an official telling you he thought he saw something, but he's not sure. When that happens, you try to get positive reinforcement, but if nobody specifically saw anything, you have no choice but to throw out the penalty.

On the other hand, sometimes you'll see things, but it's up to your own discretion whether or not to call them. This does not mean ignoring important calls—it's more like selecting what is unfair or not. Basically if something is minor and has no effect on the play, generally it is not called. Such as, if the play is a run to the right side and an offensive lineman way over on the left is holding somebody who wouldn't have a chance at making the play anyway, generally it goes unflagged.

Game Day

SEC officials are expected to be in town the night before a game. The crew gets together for dinner, and inevitably the conversation turns to officiating. It's something we all have in common and something we all love, so it's a natural progression. We get up the morning of game day, eat breakfast together, and continue talking football.

After breakfast we gather in a room to watch a tape of the previous week's officiating highlights and lowlights. It's generally about 45 minutes long and contains great calls, blown calls, questionable calls, and the like. The SEC provides the tape; the Supervisor of Officials puts it together. He collects video of things he notices as well as plays sent in by angry or appreciative coaches. He narrates it, letting us know what exactly to look for and why each play was included. The head referee is then given the tape, and he presents it to his crew. The point is not to embarrass anyone, though if there's a play you missed, it's hard to avoid that when your mistake is broadcast to all your colleagues. (On the other hand, it's a good feeling when you make a great call and everyone gets to see it again.) The main point is to learn—it's a way to provide constructive criticism. The tape is confidential, and officials are instructed not to talk about it, for obvious reasons.

Once we finish watching the tape, we return to our rooms to dress for the game. This is an SEC practice, different from most other conferences, where officials dress in rooms provided specifically for them—we put on our uniforms in our hotel rooms before we go to the game. Our idea is that the less time we spend at the stadium, the better—there's no point in fueling the fire if something controversial has happened. We use the official dressing room before the game and at halftime as a place to rest, collect our thoughts and whatnot, but not to dress. Most conferences don't work this way, but back in the days of split crews, officials from other conferences generally liked our way better.

The state troopers or police pick us up at the hotel and drive us to the game, blue lights flashing. The minute the game is over, we're in the police cruisers again, speeding back to the hotel. We're back at the hotel, out of our uniforms, cleaned up, and ready for the postgame critique before most fans are out of the stadium.

We get to the stadium about 90 minutes before kickoff. We assemble in the dressing room and make sure everybody is fine-tuned, and then the referee and the umpire visit both of the head coaches, the visiting team, and finally the home team.

The meetings with the coaches are a time for the referee and coaches to talk for a minute before the game while they are still on good terms. We go over a few things with them, the first of which is making sure our watches are synchronized so that we know exactly when kickoff will occur. If there has been a change in kickoff time, we note that and make sure everybody knows. The next thing is getting the names and numbers of the captains for introduction purposes. In the meantime, the umpire checks over any equipment that could be illegal, such as if a player has a cast, he makes sure it conforms to NCAA requirements.

This is also the time for coaches to go over unusual plays, to make sure the officials know what is coming, and to see what is legal or illegal. The coach may bring the head referee over to a blackboard with the plays drawn up and explain how they work. That generally occurs during the early part of the year if there has been a rule change or something. When I began officiating, coaches would bring up the subject themselves if there were something of hazy legality that they weren't sure about. After a couple of years, the conference began requiring officials to ask coaches if they had any unusual plays, and that's the way it was for the majority of my tenure as an official.

I did a game one time in Starkville, Mississippi, between Mississippi State and an out-of-conference team who will remain nameless. I was meeting with the visiting coach, and he took me to the chalkboard and proudly showed me a play he was planning to use. It was the "hideout," or "water-bucket" play, a purely illegal play. The way the play worked was they would huddle up with 10 players, and right before the snap, the 11th player would step on the field—completely illegal. If you wanted to draw exactly how not to do it, this guy had it.

I told him to wait a minute. "You're not going to run this play. This play is illegal," I said.

"This play isn't illegal. I ran it last week and they never called it," he replied.

"Well let me rephrase it," I said. "I can't tell you that you can't run the play, but if you run it today, there's a good chance it'll be called back and you'll be assessed a 15-yard penalty."

Much to his consternation, he didn't try the hide-out play that day.

Exactly 30 minutes before kickoff, the officials take the field. Each official has specific pregame duties assigned to his position, such as making sure the lines are marked correctly, the pylons are in the right place, the chain crew knows their duties, the scoreboard clock is working correctly, and so on. With three minutes to go, we assemble on a sideline to walk out for the coin toss, and the game is under way.

Once we are back at the hotel and cleaned up after the game, we have our postgame meeting, our debriefing, if you will. We get together with the advisor and have a fairly quick postgame critique. This is generally a fact-finding meeting, finding out what each official saw during controversial plays. If somebody blatantly missed a call during the game, we call him out on it, and see what he has to say. Again, this is not done to embarrass the official who made the bad call; it is done so that if a coach or the media wants an explanation, we can tell him why we called it the way we did.

This is what I do now. Since I retired from officiating, the SEC asked me to be an advisor of officials, and I still travel to games every weekend to observe and grade a crew of officials.

Once this meeting is over, our duties as officials are through, and we return to our other lives for another week. We go our separate ways and reconvene the next Friday in a different city. Don't ever think, however, that an official who blew a call can forget it after a week—it stays with him the rest of his life.

Counting Players on the Field

One of the unforgivable sins of officiating is miscounting a team; i.e. allowing a play to happen with 12 players on the field. I've heard all the sarcastic comments—how hard can it be to count? You would think something as simple as counting wouldn't seem too difficult; the fact is, it's one of the hardest things to do as an official.

The main reason for this is time. It's almost impossible to count players while they're in the huddle, so you have to do it between the time they break the huddle and the ball is snapped. This is generally only about a 10-second time span, if even that much. It's even shorter if they use a no-huddle offense. In that time, the referee has to (in addition to watching for any illegal pre-snap movement) count all the players on the offense, check with the umpire to make sure he has the same number, and if the umpire's number is different, count and check again. Try doing all that in 10 seconds, much less with an entire city's worth of people yelling in your direction.

For example, I'm working a game (I don't remember when, where, or who, but it's not important), and when the offense breaks the huddle, I begin to count. I count 12 players. I go ahead and throw the flag, and I check with my umpire to see what he has. He has 11. This is a problem. I begin to count again, but before I can, the center snaps the ball. I wait for the play to finish and quickly count again. This time I count 11. This is puzzling, to say the least. All I can do, however, is pick up my flag and wave off the penalty. Later on I watched a tape of the game, and sure enough there were 12 men there. It's pretty obvious too—you can tell the extra player realizes he's not supposed to be there, but he doesn't exactly know what to do. He ends up running into the end zone and trying to hide behind the goalpost. I'm sad to say that it actually worked. It fooled me, my umpire, and everyone else in the stadium.

Even in spite of the difficulty, player counting is still one of the things teams and fans take for granted. In the late 1990s, there were two games where this came into play. In both instances a team had 12 men on the field during crucial, game-deciding plays. In both instances they were not called for the infraction. In both instances the team won the game. The other team's fans to this day have not forgotten those calls—and understandably so.

Keeping Up with the Downs

Arkansas and South Carolina came into the Southeastern Conference fairly late in my career, so I don't have many stories about them. One particular game that comes to mind was the 1993 game between Tennessee and Arkansas. Overall it was an uneventful, even boring game, but it stands as the closest I ever came to losing a down.

Losing count of downs is one of the unforgivable sins of officiating, right up there with forgetting a coin for the toss or not counting players before a play. It used to be considered everyone's responsibility, but that didn't work because nobody would do it, figuring someone else would. Nowadays, the main person in charge of keeping track of downs is the head linesman, but everyone is still expected to keep track. I would do it mainly to give me one less thing to think about when announcing penalties; it gave me a little extra peace of mind. The worst down loss I ever saw was when Colorado beat Missouri on fifth down and went on to win a share of the national championship because of it.

An interesting side note: The next time you watch a football game at any level, take a look at the hands of the referee and head linesman. You'll see they have a rubber band around one, and they mess with it after almost every play. In case you don't know what they're doing, they're keeping track of the downs. There are all sorts of fancy mechanisms for keeping track of downs, in addition to the scoreboard and the sideline marker, but this simple method is used by nearly every official in the world of football. The way it works is that you take two rubber bands, tie them together so they form a kind of figure-eight pattern, with one band around the wrist and the other around a finger. Your index finger represents first down, middle finger is second, ring finger third, and your pinky finger is fourth down. This way you know what down it is, no matter what the scoreboard or the down markers on the sidelines say. It also keeps your hands free for signaling, spotting the ball, and whatever else you need to do.

Anyway, back to the story.

We're working a game between Tennessee and Arkansas at Little Rock. It's been a dull game, nothing much has happened, one of those games that threatens to lull you to sleep if you're not careful.

Arkansas has the ball somewhere in the middle of the game, the linesman looks at me and signals "third down." I look down at my rubber band, move it over, and signal "third down" back to him. Everybody is signaling "third down."

Next thing I know, however, Arkansas sends in their punting team. Arkansas is behind in the game, and I know they don't want to send in their punting team on third down. I look at the other officials, and I can tell by the looks on their faces that none of them know what's going on either.

Usually when a down is lost, it's because of confusion following a penalty. That's not the case here, my main worry is that we've all gotten lulled into a stupor and just miscounted.

I call timeout and gather all the officials together, to try to figure out what the heck is happening. I ask everybody what they have, and to a man, they all say third down. To this day I don't remember anything strange happening that would have caused any confusion.

The TV people had gone to commercial, so I go to the sideline to talk to the statistician. I had decided long before that I would not miss a down without talking to the stat folks first since they keep a detailed chart of each play and can tell me exactly what's going on. I put the headset on, and after a couple of minutes of trying to get in touch with the right guy, I finally get through to the right man. Coach Ford for Arkansas is standing beside me the whole time, bugging me, asking if I'm about to give him an extra down. It's a little embarrassing, but I swallow my pride and ask the play-by-play man, and he goes through the chart and we discover it is in fact fourth down.

I have yet to figure out how we missed that down, we talked after the game and nobody knew what happened, but that shows how easy it can be to lose a down. Had Coach Ford not sent in his punting team, we never would have known what was going on. Fortunately for us, we cleared up the situation without further embarrassment.

Keeping Up with the Score

It would be much better if somebody could make it so that the weather progression over the course of the season could be reversed. The current system is flawed and in need of improvement. The way things are right now, the hottest games of the year are the ones where the officials are in the worst shape and mostly unprepared for the weather. As the season progresses and the weather gets cooler, officials naturally get into better shape, having had several games to get our legs under us.

It's September 8, 1990, and I'm working a Tennessee-Mississippi State game in Starkville. It's a brutally hot day, one of those late summer days where nobody should be outside. The television crew has set up a thermometer on the sideline and cuts to it every now and then, and it always registers well over a hundred degrees. There's no way to truly prepare for a game like this. It's just plain dangerous to have middle-aged men running around in black striped shirts in this weather. The Mississippi State staff did a great job trying to keep us cool, bringing us water at every timeout, doing whatever they could to keep down our body temperatures.

In spite of this, I notice that my back judge (who will remain nameless in this story, though he knows who he is) keeps getting glassy-eyed. I repeatedly ask him if he is okay, and he always assures me that he's fine. At one point Tennessee runs for a touchdown of about 50 yards. Being the back judge, the touchdown put the Tennessee team right in his territory. We set the ball down for the extra point attempt and get ready for the play. I look for my friend under the goalpost, which is where he is supposed to be for the extra point, but he's standing up in his normal play position. I'm thinking this is not good—something has to be wrong.

Suddenly, just before I'm about to call an officials' timeout, he gets a puzzled look on his face and realizes they're about to kick the ball. He gets his wits about him and quickly gets into his position before Tennessee kicks the extra point. He signals the kick good, and television takes a timeout. I take this opportunity to check on him, and before I can even say a word, he looks at me and says, "That's the darnedest thing I've ever seen."

"What's the darnedest thing you've ever seen?" I ask him.

"He runs the ball 50 yards, lines up on first down, and kicks a field goal."

Now I know something's wrong. "No, it wasn't a field goal," I tell him. "That was an extra point. Did you not know he scored?"

"I had no idea," he said.

I figured this was a good time to let him rest a while and get the cobwebs out. He sat out a while and returned to the game in the second half, cooled off and refreshed.

Keeping Up with Who's Out

One thing I'm asked sometimes is what we do in the event that a fight breaks out. That's a difficult subject, as it's more of a situational thing, basically a numbers game. If it's just a couple of players getting into it, it's okay; we can usually stop it pretty well. But in the event of a bench-clearing brawl, seven officials are going to have a hard time stopping 200 adrenaline-charged men going at each other. In that case, we generally get out of there and let the police or security staff take control and restore order. The other option is just to let them fight themselves out, which usually happens after a minute or two—they just get tired of fighting.

A few years ago when a friend of mine was working a small college game, he threw player number 71 out of the game for fighting. Order was restored, and the game got back under way. There was another fight the next quarter, and it was a little more vicious this time. One of the players told an official that the instigator was the same guy he had thrown out in the last quarter. He looked at the player, who was wearing a different number this time, but looked familiar.

"Didn't I already throw you out of the game last quarter?" he asked.

"Yes sir, I just went and changed jerseys and came back. You said number 71 was ejected, so I figured if I was wearing a different number, I could come back."

So my friend threw him out again, this time making sure to point out the exact player and not just the number.

Using a Microphone

The microphone has been an interesting new development in football. When they first came into use in the 1980s, it caused a stir among referees, since most of them were not used to speaking in front of people, much less in front of tens of thousands of people. We started seeing cases of mike-fright.

There's no cue card to read when you're on the field, you're basically making things up. Guys weren't used to having to speak when signaling penalties, just waving their arms and getting on their way. This brought a whole new dimension to things, having to talk and signal at the same time.

This happened to me one time during a game between Tennessee and Florida. One team had 12 men on the field, and they all participated in the play, which made it a 15-yard penalty. So I flipped on the microphone in front of 107,000 fans and a national television audience.

"We've got . . .." I couldn't remember the rest of the sentence. I thought for a second, couldn't remember it, and turned off the mike. I figured maybe if I turned the mike on and started saying it, it would come to me. So I flipped it back on and started the sentence again.

"We've got . . .." Nothing. I was drawing a complete blank.

I figured I had to say something, tell people what was going on. I finally flipped on the mike, pointed to a sideline, and said, "We got too many players over here."

The commissioner was at the ball game that day, and he came up to me afterward. "You couldn't remember 'illegal participation,' could you?" he asked.

"Not to save my life," I responded.

When it first came into play, the microphone was only used for television games. Later it became standard for all games. I was just coming up through the ranks at the time, and I knew I'd have to use one at some point. I decided to get ready for this, and whenever I worked a scrimmage, I would go through the motions just like I had a microphone on and I was announcing it to a full stadium. I'm sure the players and coaches thought I was nuts, but it really helped me out. By the time I actually worked a television game and I had to flip on the mike, it came naturally to me.

It seems like every game has some sort of trouble with the microphone, either feedback or just plain cutting out—the mike always seems to mess up. I always tried to circumvent that. When the guy from the stadium or the TV network would bring me the mike and the wireless pack, I would always make sure to test it myself, by walking out to the 50-yard line, flipping it on, and making sure it worked. They would always protest, saying they had tested it and everything, but I wanted to see for myself. You'd be surprised how many times I got out there, and nothing came out of the speakers. I'd get a blank look from the sound guy, as well as an "I don't know, it worked before . . .."

It also can cause some confusion when you are piped over the PA system since there's a delay between when you talk into the microphone and when the sound comes back to you. If you start trying to listen to what you're saying, a lot of times you'll end up sounding really funny. You have to ignore the speakers, say your piece, and turn the mike off to avoid feedback.

Grading

There used to be something called a "strike list" in the SEC. Every year, before the season started, the coaches had a chance to name up to three officials in each position they didn't want working their games. This could be done for a variety of reasons: personality conflict, a series of bad calls, even superstition came into play on occasion. The interesting thing was that most coaches never used it. On a rare occasion there was a bad call that a coach just couldn't let go, and he would choose to stay away from that official for a year or so, but it had to be a really terrible call for a coach to strike him. There were even a couple of coaches who struck officials just because their team seemed to lose every time that official called one of their games. The officials were not privy to the list—the only way we could figure out who had been struck was by patterns. If a certain school didn't appear on your schedule for a couple of years, you'd start to get suspicious.

I'm glad to say the strike list doesn't exist anymore. The coaches have tried over the years to remove themselves from the decision-making process in terms of officials. The idea is if you're good enough to officiate in the Southeastern Conference, you're good enough to call any conference game.

There are, however, a lot of restrictions as to who can officiate for which teams in the SEC. It follows basic conflict-of-interest rules. If you went to a school or have a child who plays there, you can't officiate for that school. If you played for a coach, you can't work his games. This also works for out-of-conference schools. Since I went to Georgia Tech, I was never allowed to call one of their games even though they were not in the SEC. Even though this seems like simple logic, there are a few conferences that do not subscribe to these rules. I won't name them, but in some places, if you were an All-American quarterback for a university, you can still work a game there. I feel that puts too much pressure on the people involved since officiating is done mostly by instinct instead of by thinking about the play.

Ever turned 107,000 people against you in a split second? It's a scary feeling. Most people don't understand that officials are accountable for the calls they make. They seem to think we leave the game and that's it. This could not be further from the truth. We are accountable to the Southeastern Conference, and I will get to that in a minute. The main person an official is accountable to, in any sport, is himself. If an official makes a bad call and realizes it, it eats at him, especially if it is important to the outcome of the game. I promise you the offended coaches, players, and fans are not hurt nearly as much as the official who blew the call. He will never get it out of his mind. Eventually the fans will forget it, for the most part, but it will stay with him to his dying day. It's an unfortunate thing I've noticed: You never remember the great calls you made, just the few you really messed up. You never get over the nagging feelings of "if I had done this differently I could have seen it." Now in the case of judgment calls—those that could go either way and you just call what you see—those you don't worry about. In that case you simply remember you're the best official the SEC could find for that position on that particular day, and you made the call based on what you saw. You let it go and move on. It's the cut-and-dried ones that you just flat-out missed that haunt you.

It was easier in the days before the giant screens. Those are a mixed blessing, but I would be lying if I said no official ever stole a glance at one after a close play. On one hand, if it was a bang-bang play and you got it right, it serves as a sort of instant vindication. But just as frequently it causes you to get booed twice, even louder the second time as people who didn't catch it the first time get to see your mistake in slow motion from angles you wish you had. They never cheer the good calls, but they make sure you know when you mess up.

Officials are independent contractors, hired by the Southeastern Conference, but are not employees. We are held accountable by the SEC, and they determine the standards we must uphold in order to continue working for them.

Imagine getting four grades for your performance every time you showed up for work. That's what it's like to be a Southeastern Conference official. After every game, we get four independent grades: one from the observer at the game, one each from the home and visiting coaches, and a film grade the following Monday. The crew also gets graded as a whole. The grades used to be published in a book for all to see at the end of the season. The book was kept confidential by SEC officials, but everyone within the officiating fraternity knew how everyone else was doing. Today it's even more confidential; you are told your own score and where you placed, but not how anyone else did or where they placed.

These grades aren't just arbitrary, meaningless numbers; they are used for several purposes. The grades are mostly used to figure out who gets rewarded with post-season duties. The Southeastern Conference Championship game is officiated by the crew of officials that gets the best overall score. Bowl games are done differently.

The NCAA allots the SEC a certain amount of games to officiate, loosely proportionate to the number of teams it has placed in bowls. If they put six teams in bowl games, then the SEC will officiate three games. These games are not officiated by a specific crew; instead, the SEC ranks officials based on who scores the highest at each position, and from there they pick groups to go to the different bowl games. These are picked in order of importance. If the SEC is given the Rose Bowl, it will get the highest graded official at each position, essentially giving them an SEC all-star crew. The next highest bowl gets whoever was number two at their position and so on. It's a reward system for a job well done.

On the other hand, I've seen people get consistently bad grades for long enough that they were dismissed from the SEC altogether. This is rare, considering the intense screening process involved with becoming an SEC official, but it does happen.

Chapter 2

The Coin Toss

And then there's the coin toss. I've been doing speaking engagements for years, and one point I always made was that whenever I got around to writing a book, I'd devote one whole chapter to the coin toss and one to Coach Bryant. Well, here's the first one.

It is always interesting to see people's reactions when I tell them I'm going to do a whole chapter on the coin toss. The looks on their faces range from consternation to confusion. It's strange, yes, but it's true; the coin toss is the most exciting part of a football game. It's the point where anyone can win. I've been in games where emotions were running so high that players got into a fistfight before they even met for the coin toss. The game is up for grabs; the players are nervous, the coaches are nervous, the officials are anxious to get things going, and absolutely anything can happen.

It's a difficult time to be an official as well. This may seem strange, since all we are supposed to do is introduce the players, ask whether the visiting team wants heads or tails, flip the coin, and ask the winner of the coin toss what they want. The problem is that at that point in the game, there is so much confusion going on that things can get pretty hairy. The head coach is worried about every possible factor in the game: field condition, temperature, wind, game plan, anything that can have an effect on the game. He sort of remembers what he told the captain. The captain is nervous about the game; all he wants to do is get the game under way so the butterflies will get out of his stomach. He's pretty sure he remembers what the coach wants. The same thing is going on across the field on the other sideline. It's my job to sort all this mess out and figure out what each team wants without coaching them or helping them.

Nobody paid much attention to coin toss protocol until the NFL game between Pittsburgh and Detroit where Jerome Bettis of the Steelers called "tails" for the overtime coin toss, the referee heard "heads," and Detroit got the ball and won the game with a field goal. I guess I anticipated something of that sort, so I was prepared for it. My method was to catch the coin but cover it with my hand. I repeat the choice back to the player to make sure we are in agreement, and then I uncover it. If I don't catch it or if I drop it, I flip it again. This prevents any misunderstanding from occurring.

This was especially difficult since several games, including a lot of bowl games, have special coins minted specifically for that game. One coin I still have was minted for a game between Florida and Tennessee on September 20, 1997. It has a Florida Gator on one side and a Tennessee logo on the other. There was no specific head or tail to the coin, and to call one side heads would mean insulting the other side. Peyton Manning was captain of Tennessee's squad that year, and without thinking I asked him which side of the coin he wanted to pick, Tennessee or Florida. He looked at me and said "Mr. Burleson, you've got to be kidding."

Most referees have a specific coin they use at every game, and I was no exception. I had a silver coin I carried to every game starting in my high-school days and continuing throughout my officiating career. It became sort of a good-luck coin for me. It's a special silver coin with a football on one side that was minted for the centennial of high-school football, and it was given to me by the National Federation of High Schools. I still have it to this day. It never happened to me, but you'd be surprised how many times a referee will walk to midfield with nothing in his pocket to flip. It's about the most embarrassing thing that can happen to a referee, standing there trying to find something to flip, asking people if they have any change. I've seen people use all kinds of things, rocks, pieces of paper, anything with two distinct sides.

That's only the first part, however, and also probably the easiest. The first thing I ask once the coin is flipped is if they want to defer their choice to the second half. Most teams do. Then there are three choices: kick off, receive, or defend a goal. That creates a bit of a dilemma.

My first game of the 1982 season was between Memphis State (now the University of Memphis) and Ole Miss, on September 4, 1982. The two schools are near each other and recruit the same area, so it's a pretty heated rivalry. It's a sweltering summer day. A cold front had tried to come through the area, but the only thing it could muster was a hot, stiff wind.

Steve Sloan is the head coach at Ole Miss, and while we are waiting to walk to midfield, I overhear him talking to his captain. "Son, I want to tell you one more time," he says. "I want to make sure you understand that if we win the toss, we want the wind. Understand me?" The player acknowledges that he does.

We go to midfield for the toss. I can see the wheels turning in the player's head as he walks; there's something he's trying to figure out. I figured out his thought process later. He goes over possible scenarios and realizes that if they take the wind, they'll end up kicking off, so that's what he has to do. This was probably true. We get to midfield, I flip the coin, and he wins.

"Ok, you won the toss," I say. "You have three choices: kick off, receive, or defend a goal." I emphasized the last part (there was no "defer" choice in 1982).

"We want to kick off," he says. His coach told him specifically to take the wind. There's a problem here. I try to correct him as subtly as I can.

"Are you sure?" I ask. He nods his head. I realize there's no hope, so I turn to the Memphis captain. "You're receiving, but you also get your choice of which goal to defend." He looks around for a second.

"I'll take the wind, Sir," he says.

So I line them up and signal that Memphis is receiving and which goal each team will defend, and we break. Everybody goes to their place, and I start walking to my post. Before I get anywhere, I feel a hand on my shoulder. I turn around to see the Ole Miss captain with a look of puzzlement on his face.

"Mr. Burleson, don't leave me just yet, please."

"What's the problem?" I ask him.

"Let me make sure I understand this. I won the toss, right?"

"That's right."

"I lost the ball and the wind?"

I said yes.

"Coach Sloan ain't gonna like this," he said.

"I hate to say it, but that's the first thing you've gotten right so far," I said.

Ole Miss won the game, but the next day in the paper, Coach Sloan was quoted as saying "Well, we won the game, but we've got to work on our coin toss."

They say you learn something new every day. Just when I thought I knew everything there was to know about college football rules, I was proven wrong.

I'm working a game between Georgia and Vanderbilt at Athens. Vandy sends their All-American kicker out to handle the toss. I toss the coin, Vanderbilt wins. "Son, you've won the toss," I say to the kicker. "You can kick off, receive, or defend the goal."

He looks at me, with a serious look on his face. "You know what? I don't wanna do any of those," he says.

"Well, I don't know of another one, besides the three I gave you." I tell him. I know Vandy kids are supposed to be smart, but I've been working football games for 20 years, and I'm pretty sure I haven't missed anything.

"Yes, Sir, there's another one. Coach told me another one."

"Well I'd be interested to know what it is."

"He told me to take the wind."

Now I had already told him he could choose to defend a goal, so I tell him: "Now this might come as a big surprise, but that's one of the options I gave you. You can defend a goal." I wait for him to tell me what he wants.

He, in turn, waits for me to tell him something else.

This is a televised game, and after a few seconds pass, the television crew starts to get antsy. They want to know what's going on. I start trying to figure out how to get out of this mess. The Vandy kicker looks at me.

"Is there something else I'm supposed to tell you?" he asks.

"Yes, you need to tell me which end of the field you want to defend."

He looks at me funny. "Which end of the field?"

I realize this is getting nowhere. "Let me sum it up for you. Tell me which way the wind is blowing, and I'll figure out which end of the field you want."

A look of panic crosses his face, followed by a grave seriousness. "You know what? Coach didn't tell me which way the wind was blowing," says the All-American kicker from Vanderbilt.

Chapter 3

The Rules

I have always had a keen interest in the rules of sports. The fine points and intricacies of football and basketball rules have always intrigued me. I had some friends in high school who shared this interest, and sometimes we would play games to see if we could stump each other on obscure rules and penalties. My roommate at Tech, Jerry Shurbet, a very good Tech player and the best man at my wedding, was great at this game.

The NCAA rulebook is an ever-evolving process, with new rules coming and going every year. These days, things are pretty much stable; most of the changes are little nitpicky things to clear up ambiguous rule interpretations. These are voted on by the NCAA rules committee at their annual winter meeting.

People ask me about rules all the time, wondering why we created the celebration rule, the fair catch rule, etc., and I have to explain that officials do not make the rules. The rules committee is made up entirely of active coaches with one supervisor. There are no officials on the rules committee. We are simply the policemen, there to enforce rules with no say in creating or changing them. However, that being said, over the course of my career, I was involved in three games that resulted in rules changes at the end of the year.

The first is a game between Mississippi State and Auburn at Jordan-Hare Stadium in Auburn in 1981. Auburn has the ball near midfield with the game all but won. Time is running out, fourth down and short, if Auburn makes a first down the game is essentially over. They come up to the line as if they're going to go for it. Their plan, however, is simply to wait and see if they can get the defense to jump offside, giving them the first down. The quarterback barks out the signals, trying to instigate movement.

The plan works, and a defensive end jumps. He quickly realizes the error of his ways and gets back to the line. He is successful, and having avoided contact, is legally back onside. The Auburn center sees this and tries to snap the ball to catch the end in the act. He isn't quite positive of this decision, and he skips the ball a little bit while contemplating whether or not to snap it.

This was an illegal snap. At the time it is not a dead ball foul, simply a 5-yard penalty. The ball is live, and the play goes on.

So he snaps the ball to catch the defensive end offside, but the end had gotten back in time. Head linesman George Morris, my friend and a great Georgia Tech player, throws a flag for the illegal snap. The Auburn quarterback is not expecting the snap and has trouble with it. A Mississippi State lineman sees this and knocks the quarterback to the ground. The play is dead, and the Auburn players start celebrating the offsides penalty, which will ensure them the win. Problem is, there was no player offsides. The penalty is for the illegal snap, which is 5 yards and a replay of the down. Since the play actually started, however, the down counts; and since it was fourth down, Mississippi State has the option of declining the penalty and taking the ball. They decline the penalty, take the ball at midfield, and drive for the winning touchdown.

Not surprisingly, a lot of people were unhappy about that play. It would be the last of its kind in college football, though, as the NCAA ruled an illegal snap a dead ball at the end of the season, which it should have been all along.

The second game is in September 1985, UCLA at Tennessee. It is early in the season, the first or second game for both teams. The first time UCLA lines up on defense, Tennessee sends three receivers out toward their sideline. They had sent in a substitute for the play, so there are 12 men on the field. The rules at the time state only that you can't have 12 men on the field during the play, nothing else. UCLA sends out three defenders to cover the flankers. Just before the snap, the player closest to the sideline steps off the field, leaving the man who had been covering him alone, way over near the sideline. As you might expect, this leaves another Tennessee player uncovered. The quarterback zips the ball to him, and they make about 30 yards on the play.

A couple of plays later, they run this play again and make another huge gain. I finally have to call a timeout, and I walk over to the Tennessee sideline to talk to Coach Majors. At the time, there is no rule specifically prohibiting such an action, but there is one about using a substitute to deceive. Though they are not using the substitute himself to do this, I have to stop it somehow. I tell Coach Majors that though this is a gray area and there's nothing specifically preventing them from doing it, I will be interpreting the rule to say they can't. They refrain from using that play for the rest of the game, but the damage has already been done. Tennessee gets a touchdown on that drive, and the game ends in a tie.

At the end of that year, the NCAA Rules Committee changed the regulations to prohibit this action. Over the years the rule has evolved to where teams may not have more than 11 players when they break the huddle.

Ever wonder why it's not intentional grounding when a quarterback spikes the ball to stop the clock? It used to be. That all changed after a game in October 1989 between Florida and LSU in Baton Rouge.

It's relatively early in the season. Mike Archer is LSU's coach, and Galen Hall is at the helm for Florida in what will turn out to be his final game. LSU has not had a particularly good year up to this point, and the natives are getting restless.

The game is tied and almost over. Florida has the ball around LSU's 40-yard line with no timeouts. Time was running out, and they had no way to stop the clock. Florida sends their All-American running back Emmitt Smith around end, with orders to get out of bounds and stop the clock. He makes a pretty good gain but is unable to get out of bounds. The clock continues to run and drops below 10 seconds. The Florida quarterback gets everybody lined up, gets the snap, and flings the ball over the LSU coach's head.

I watch the ball cross the sideline, with the scoreboard clock in the corner of my eye. The ball lands out of bounds with a couple of seconds left on the clock, but the clock operator has to wait for the signal to stop the clock. By the time we react and signal and he hits the button, time has expired. The LSU sideline goes nuts, as do 80,000 fans; a tie is better than a loss.

I know there should be time left on the clock. I can't leave that stadium knowing I didn't give both teams a fair chance. I keep the teams off the field and go talk to my clock operator. He explains that he stopped the clock when he saw the signal and that the call could go either way in his opinion. So I go to midfield, where the rest of the officials are standing. Butch Lambert Jr., the umpire, looks at me and says, "I don't know what you're about to do, Dick, but I don't believe it's gonna be real popular." He is right. I instruct the clock operator to put one second back on the clock. I go to both sidelines, explaining that time was left on the clock after the pass was incomplete so I'm putting that time back on the clock. This decision is wildly unpopular among the vast majority of people in that stadium, but I know it is the right one.

To attempt the game-winning kick, Florida sends in a kicker who has never attempted a field goal in his college career. I don't remember how far this kick is, but it is a good distance. The chances are slim that he will make it. LSU decides to ice him a bit and calls a timeout.

One of the youngest officials in my crew, a back judge named Prince Pollard, comes up to me during the timeout, clapping his hands. He says, "Dick, I think you did exactly right. I know there was time left. I saw it myself. I know there was time left on the clock."

"Well I'm glad you agree with me," I reply, "because in a minute they're gonna try what could be the winning field goal, and you're gonna be under the goalpost to rule whether or not the kick is good."

The smile on his face fades a bit as he begins contemplating his fate. He slowly turns to walk away. I stop him. "Oh, and let me remind you of one other thing," I say. "I am on the 50-yard line."

He looks puzzled. I continue. "I am only 50 yards from the tunnel. You, on the other hand, are a hundred yards from it." The smile completely disappears, and he walks back to the end zone slowly, looking around at the multitude of already unhappy LSU fans.

As fate would have it, the Florida kicker wins the game with his first-ever collegiate field-goal attempt. The kick is straight down the middle, but from my vantage point 50 yards away, I can't quite tell if it makes it over the crossbar. I see my young friend slowly raise his hands to signal "good." I have already begun making my way off the field, but I have to stop briefly to make the signal.

Before I can even get my hands down, some sort of blur whizzes by me, nearly bowling me over in the process. It takes me a second to regain my composure and figure out what it is. I look in the direction it was going and see my friend Prince Pollard, who has already made it halfway across the field and is practically setting the grass on fire hightailing it to the tunnel.

The game was not televised so there were no instant replays to back me up on that call. Sometime the following week, however, the people who put together highlight tapes of LSU games did a superimposition of the play and the game clock, and it showed clearly that the call was correct. I felt much better after that. Even though I was still persona non grata in Baton Rouge, I felt vindicated.

Since new rules are picked up or dropped every year, things can get confusing for those of us trying to keep up with them. There have been times where a new rule has been instituted only to be eliminated the next year and brought back the year after. Not having a copy of the rulebook on the field, sometimes it's hard to remember which way the rule goes at a certain time. You're forced to fly by the seat of your pants. Here's an example. This one sticks in my mind pretty well; it's the only time I can recall where I know for a fact I made a rules mistake.

I'm working the Tennessee-Georgia game in Athens, Georgia, in 1994. Somewhere in the third quarter there was a penalty involving offensive pass interference. The penalty for this was 15 yards. In the years before, it had also included loss of down, but this had been removed before this season started. I forgot about this and went by the previous year's rule and gave them a loss of down as well. I never gave it a thought, and nobody else seemed to notice this; everybody simply went about their business.

Generally if you make a bad call or a rules mistake, the coaches for the team receiving the erroneous penalty go crazy and don't let up until you relent. I guess everybody deferred to my judgment because nothing happened, and the game simply went on. The play didn't affect the outcome of the game, but I couldn't relax until I figured out whether it was right or not. I checked the rulebook later and found out I had in fact made an incorrect call. Even though it had no effect on the game, that call bugs me to this day.

Chapter 4

Great SEC Football Players

A lot of people ask me who I consider to be the greatest players I ever officiated for. That's nearly impossible to say. Working in the SEC afforded me the luxury of working alongside some of the finest athletes ever to play the game, and to try to pick the best of them would be a daunting task, to say the least. I can, however, talk about some players who have had a profound effect on me in one way or another.

I was fortunate to work in the SEC during the early 1980s, which meant I got to see Herschel Walker and Bo Jackson in action. They were probably the biggest marquee names I had during my 25 years, and for good reason. They were simply amazing to watch—there's not much I can really say that would do them justice except to say they were exceptional athletes, and I was lucky to have had the opportunity to watch them up close.

In October 1980 I work my first game with Herschel Walker. He has been highly touted all season, and I want to see what the fuss is all about. I find out early in the first quarter. I'm right behind him as he runs around end and cuts upfield. This was one of his first college games, but he's already built like an NFL running back. Just as he turns upfield, a nice-size hole opens up for him. He bursts through the hole like a freight train. The only thing between him and the goal line is a single Kentucky defensive back. The look on that young man's face is priceless as he sees Herschel barreling toward him, and he realizes he has to figure out a way to stop him. Herschel doesn't try to sidestep him or fake him out; he just tries to run right over him. To his credit, the defensive back actually does bring him down, hanging on by one foot as he is dragged about 25 yards.

There were other players I just had a special rapport with who were captains for several years or just played in a lot of games I worked. I could never comment on my "favorite" players, but there were some I just had a great respect for and connection with. The first two who come to mind are Jay Barker, the Alabama quarterback, and Kurt Crain, the linebacker from Auburn. They were both just great people and were a pleasure to work with.

One game I really remember vividly was the 1982 Nebraska-Auburn game at Jordan-Hare Stadium. Nebraska came in ranked number 6 and was the first major intersectional game ever played at Auburn. Nebraska's running back was Mike Rozier, who would go on to win the Heisman Trophy the next year.

Chapter 5

Coach Paul "Bear" Bryant

As I said in Chapter 2 about the coin toss, when I give speeches I always say, "I'll have to devote a whole chapter to Coach Bryant." Well, here it is.

Coach Paul Bryant and my father were good friends, as my father had been the university's engineering consultant when the first athletic expansion and upgrade program occurred. Coach Bryant knew my father from past meetings, and when he commissioned the facilities to be built, he called my father in to watch out for the university's interests. My father oversaw the renovation of Denny Stadium and the construction of Bryant Hall, the first athletic dormitory, and Coleman Coliseum, as well as other renovations and facility upgrades.

I don't know if he had anything to do with my selection into the SEC, but I learned later that my father had told Coach Bryant about me when I was still officiating in the Gulf South Conference. He told the Coach I would be applying to move up into the SEC soon, and he would appreciate it if Coach Bryant would give whatever help he could to me. Coach Bryant told my father he was pretty sure he had met all of his children when they had come through the university and would be glad to help. My father told him he hadn't met this one since he didn't attend the University of Alabama. Coach Bryant was taken aback. How could Joe Burleson have a child not attend The University? Where did he go to school? My father told him I went to Georgia Tech. He might as well have said Auburn, as Tech was directly below them on Coach Bryant's blacklist. The look on the Coach's face was of a man betrayed. Nevertheless, he liked my father and promised to help out if the opportunity presented itself.

This was the way it worked in those days; it helped greatly to have somebody sponsor your efforts to become an SEC official. I just happened to have the best. At the time, the selection committee for officials was comprised of three active officials and three active coaches, who rotated on and off the committee every three years. Coach Bryant was not on the committee when I was selected, but I don't know what influence he may have had on the committee at the time. Nevertheless, I wouldn't have been considered for selection if my performance had not merited it, so I never worried about it.

I mentioned earlier that the head referee meets with both head coaches before every game to discuss captains, synchronize watches, and whatever else needs to be covered before the game. One thing that set Coach Bryant apart from the rest was that no matter who the head referee was, at every pregame meeting he would put something into that referee's mind that was to his benefit. As a referee, you knew it was coming—it was just a matter of when. With me he was fairly consistent. The first thing he would do as soon as I entered the locker room was to remind me that he and my father were very close friends, and the bigger the game, the better friends they had been.

I learned quickly that Coach Bryant was not someone to be taken lightly. He was a whole lot sharper than he let on.

"Set My Watch for Me."

Sometime in my first years in the SEC, while I'm still working freshman games, I am called to run the clock for a game between Alabama and Ole Miss at Legion Field. The head referee is Jimmy Artley, from Savannah, Georgia. A great referee and a super guy, we would become friends over the years. At this time, senior referees exclusively work higher profile games—there is no rotation. Therefore, Coach Bryant sees Jimmy several times a year, and they know each other well. Jimmy knows I am a head referee and that I am new to the league, so he invites me along for his meetings with the head coaches, to see how he does it. The idea is that whomever I work with next week will also invite me along, so I can learn how different referees work. This is a big deal to a budding young official like myself, and I jump at the chance to get a behind-the-scenes look at a big-time referee in action.

As we walk across the turf at Legion Field toward the locker rooms, Artley explains another reason why he wants me to accompany him. "Dick, one of the reasons I want you to go with me today is that I have to set time with Coach Bryant and the Ole Miss coach," he says.

"I'm aware of that," I reply.

"I have to wear bifocals. I don't like to wear them during a game because they bother me. My normal vision is fine; just when things get up real close, I need a little help. So I don't wear my bifocals during the game; I don't even have them with me. Consequently I can't read my watch. So I want you to get right up behind me when I'm talking to Coach Bryant, and when I raise up my watch, I just want you to whisper the time into my ear."

This seems strange to me, but he is a well-respected senior referee, so I defer to his seniority and agree to go along with the plan. I figure this is what he does for every game.

We get to the locker room, and I meet Coach Bryant for the first time in an official capacity. He hasn't figured out whose son I am so I stay in the back and don't say anything. This being the first game of the year, they commence to talking about fishing, each other's families, anything and everything but the game at hand. Finally Artley gets things down to business.

"Okay, Coach, I need your captain's name and number."

Coach Bryant gives it to him. I know what is coming next so I walk up behind Artley.

"Alright, now we need to set time. I have . . .." and he holds up his watch.

It is a night game. "Six-fifteen," I whisper.

"Six-fifteen," says Jimmy Artley.

Coach Bryant doesn't say anything for a couple of seconds, just blinks his eyes and stares at Artley. He cocks his head to one side and looks at me. The ruse has obviously failed, but Coach is going to play it for all it is worth. He looks around and then down at his watch. A smile creeps across his lips. He calmly takes off his watch, hands it to Artley, and says, "You know, Jim, I have to wear bifocals. I can't set my watch without them. I ain't got my bifocals with me. How 'bout you go ahead and set my watch for me."

Coach Bryant at Neyland Stadium

My very next experience with Coach Bryant is while I was still working the clock. Alabama was playing Tennessee at Neyland Stadium. Alabama had a great team, and the game figured to be a blowout. Nevertheless Coach Bryant was nervous—he was always anxious before games, especially against teams like Tennessee and Auburn.

I'm on the sideline with Coach Bryant, with the scoreboard clock control in my hand, and one of the local high-school football coaches is in charge of feeding me cable as I need it and making sure it doesn't get tangled or caught on anything.

Nowadays scoreboard-clock controls use very small cables that don't get in the way. In 1974, though, the cable is much larger, like a coaxial television cable. One of the ancillary duties of the clock operator is to keep the previous spot after a play is over. This is done in case something happens like a punt that goes 45 yards but is called back for a penalty, you can find the previous spot even if the chains have moved.

Tennessee kicks off to Alabama to start the game. I try to anticipate where the ball will end up after the kickoff so I can get the spot marked quickly. I do, and play begins. On the first play from scrimmage, Alabama makes a considerable gain. I begin to walk to the next spot but the cord catches me and won't move. I look back and the guy feeding me cable is pulling on it, trying to get it unstuck from whatever is holding it back. Looking beyond him, I see that Coach Bryant is standing on the cable.

On the next play Alabama fumbles, and Tennessee gets the ball at about the 10-yard line. Neyland Stadium goes berserk. Coach Bryant is livid, but he doesn't get off the cord. I desperately need to get to the spot of the ball. I'm pulling, the cable feeder is pulling, but we can't get him off the cable. The cable feeder gets an idea.

"I'll get him off it," he says, then proceeds to grab the box and yank it as hard as he can. Coach Bryant doesn't budge, and the cable doesn't either. What does move, however, is the control box. The cable snaps in two right where it plugs into the box, rendering the box and the scoreboard clock useless.

I don't notice this at first; I'm too busy focusing on the next play. I run to the next spot and flip the switch to stop the clock and nothing happens, it just keeps running. I look back and there's the cable puller frantically trying to tie the broken ends of the cable together, of course to no avail.

So we end up with a full-scale mess on our hands. There is no scoreboard clock so I have to keep time on the field, giving updates to the coaches every so often. Coach Bryant does his best to drive me nuts, asking me how much time is left after nearly every play. He has a big lead and wants the game to be over. At one point he asks how much time is left, I tell him four and a half minutes. He just scowls and yells: "You told me that 10 minutes ago!"

Covering Crowd Noise

My next story about Coach Bryant comes in 1979.

I'm the head referee for a night game at Legion Field between Baylor and Alabama early in September. This is the last of Coach Bryant's national championship teams, and Baylor is sorely outclassed. Alabama ends up winning 45-0, and at no point is the game in doubt.

Nevertheless, when I go to the locker room for the pregame meeting, Coach Bryant is his usual nervous self. He stops pacing to talk to me about my father and to remind me what good friends they are. We go through the motions, naming captains, synchronizing watches, and checking equipment, and once we are done I wish him good luck and we begin to leave. As I'm walking out the door, Coach Bryant stops me.

"Mr. Burleson, you forgot something," he says.

I carried a card with me to every game so that I could write down the names and numbers of the captains for each team. On the back I made a checklist of all the things I wanted to cover in the meetings. I looked down this list, and nothing was missing. "Well, Coach, I've covered everything on my list, what else needs to be done?" I ask him.

"You didn't cover crowd noise."

There's going to be 70-odd thousand Alabama fans at this game, versus about 10 people from Baylor—why could he possibly want me to cover crowd noise? At first I think he's joking, but no smile appears on his face. Looking past him, however, I can see Alabama's quarterback Steadman Shealy, and he's grinning slyly from ear to ear. Now I think I'm being set up.

There's nothing I can really do to get out of it, however, so I walk over to Steadman Shealy and tell him the procedures in case these 10 people get out of hand. I tell him he needs to know this because he will be playing in Baton Rouge and Knoxville and other hostile environments and he needs to know what to do in case it gets out of hand.

I finish telling him what to do and leave the dressing room, still puzzled by the strange request. The umpire for the game was a very experience official, a veteran of years in the league and many Bryant-coached games. "Could you believe that?" I said. "Why in the world would he want me to cover crowd noise?"

"He didn't," the umpire replied, "he wanted to know if you knew the exact procedure. It was a test."

"Wow, that had never dawned on me," I said.

"Well, you're a fairly young referee, and he wanted to know if you knew it in case we're working his game in Baton Rouge or somewhere and he needs to use it."

Coach Bryant's Last Game in Tuscaloosa

The last game I officiated for Coach Bryant was his last game at Bryant-Denny Stadium, a 38-29 loss to a very good Southern Mississippi team on November 13, 1982. He hadn't announced his retirement yet, and nobody knew exactly how ill he was.

I could tell something was wrong that day though. He just wasn't himself. He must have already been very sick because he was completely different than the man I was used to; he was subdued, quiet, and reserved. The umpire and I talked about it after our pregame meeting, how he didn't carry on any conversation besides the bare minimum, when generally he liked to chat a while before getting down to business.

He announced his retirement soon after that game. When he did, I got to thinking, and I realized that I had a lot of things signed by great coaches, but I had nothing signed by Coach Bryant. I went to *The Birmingham News* and talked to some of the sportswriters and photographers I knew there, and asked if I could look through the shots of that Southern Miss game to find one with myself and Coach Bryant in it. They told me I was welcome to look through and try to find one. I finally found one, showing a player running with the ball, me hot on his trail, and Coach Bryant watching from the sideline.

I got a print made from that picture and kept it on my desk for a while, thinking I would make it to Tuscaloosa to get him to sign it. After a while it became clear I wasn't going to make it down there anytime soon, so I decided to mail it to Coach Bryant. I sent it on a Friday, with a little note asking him to sign it for me. He died the next week, and I figured the picture to be lost and I had missed my opportunity. Imagine my surprise when the photo showed up in my mailbox the day after he died, signed and dated. On it he wrote "To Dick Burleson, a great official with class." This was one of the greatest compliments Coach Bryant could give a person. The date on the photograph is the day he had his heart attack. I talked to his secretary a few weeks later, and as it turns out, not only did I get my photograph back, but she said it was the last photograph Coach Bryant ever signed.

A famous quote of Coach Bryant's referred to how he figured if he ever quit coaching he wouldn't last much longer. He never did. The day he was buried, I received a letter in the mail from Coach Bryant, saying he was happy to sign the photo for me but that the picture showed exactly why he retired—he was criticizing the player for the way he held the football.

Michelle Meets Coach Bryant

Through his work on the improvements to the University of Alabama campus, my father came to be good friends with both Coach Bryant and his wife, Mary Harmon. I don't know how they met, but he had known the Coach for years. He became close friends with Mary Harmon Bryant through his work on Bryant Hall, the athletic dormitory. Bryant Hall was her pet project, and she would show up around lunchtime almost every day, and would sit down and have lunch with him, just to see how things were going.

As I said before, my father was an officer in the Army, and the constant traveling took a toll on his relationship with my mother, such that they were divorced when I was very young. While he was serving in World War II, he met a young lady named Michelle who was working with the French Underground against the Germans. They fell in love and got married, and after the war she came to America and has lived in Tuscaloosa ever since.

One day she told my father that she wanted to meet Coach Bryant. She had never met him and figured if she lived in the same city as a celebrity of his stature, she should get to meet him, especially if my father was friends with him. My father told her to come over at lunch and he would introduce the two of them. It was a rainy day; a steady downpour had drenched the entire town that morning, but had eased up by noon. My father was standing outside the football offices talking with Coach Bryant when Michelle showed up. When she tried to stop the car, she hit a mud puddle and skidded a few feet, splattering Coach Bryant from head to toe with mud and water. She got out of the car, terribly embarrassed and apologizing profusely, but the Coach would have none of it. "Little lady," he said, "do you honestly think that I've never had mud on me before?"

And so she and Coach Bryant were introduced, and he gave her one of his trademark houndstooth hats.

Chapter 6

Great SEC Football Coaches

I approached this chapter with some trepidation. I knew that after having a whole chapter devoted to Coach Bryant, I needed to include others as well, but I wasn't sure how to handle it. I wanted to include every school in the SEC to make sure no one was left out. I also want to speak candidly, give some insight as to what coaches are like from an official's perspective but without offending anyone.

The difficulty with doing this is that fans of SEC football are fiercely proud of their coaches. They don't want anything negative said about them, and for good reason—by simply writing a chapter on this topic, I run the risk of alienating a large segment of the audience. I hope I can avoid that while remaining true to my original intent.

There is a great deal of mutual respect between football coaches and officials. We realize how difficult each other's jobs are and the amount of skill involved in doing it well. To my knowledge, I never called a coach, head or assistant, by his first name. I always referred to them as "Coach _____." The men who coach Southeastern

Conference football are some of the best football minds out there. If they weren't, they wouldn't have the job.

I worked in the SEC for 25 years. During that time, the SEC went through 54 coaches. That averages out to more than two coaching changes a year. That's a lot of coaches. I have decided to choose one from each school that stood out to me the most in some way. This wasn't easy, as there have been some real characters at each school over the years. Nevertheless, I have picked one from each, and here they are, in alphabetical order by school.

Alabama: Gene Stallings (1990-1996)

From an officiating standpoint, there's no other way to put it: Gene Stallings was the toughest. He was far and away the most difficult coach I have ever officiated for. I feel vindicated in saying this because he says it all the time now. In his opinion, any flag thrown against the University of Alabama was wrong, period. He didn't mean it unkindly or as an affront to an official's abilities, that was just the way he saw things. An Alabama defensive lineman could sack the quarterback before the ball was even snapped, and if you threw a flag, you were going to hear about it.

If you still don't follow me, I have one other point to offer: Coach Stallings was the only coach I ever had get mad at us at a scrimmage. I don't remember what it was, but we called something against the offense in a spring scrimmage one time, some sort of drive-killing penalty, and he absolutely blew his top. We just stood there with our mouths open, not sure what to say.

He's also the only coach I've ever known who sent his players to me as messengers. Since my position was in the middle of the field and the only officials he could get to personally were the sideline officials, he would deliver messages via his players. After a controversial call, whenever I would see a player coming off the Alabama sideline toward me, I knew he had a message from Coach Stallings.

That being said however, I do have to say this. From any other aspect, Gene Stallings is one of the finest human beings I have ever known. I worked closely with him during his tenure at Alabama since I lived so close to Tuscaloosa. I was the first person he would call for practices, scrimmages, rules clinics, anytime he needed an official. He always called me "General," and he handled himself with the utmost class and dignity.

I was sitting in his office one day before conducting a rules clinic for his team, just talking about things, and I said to him, "You know, there's not a week that goes by without someone asking me what it's like to work with Coach Stallings."

He leaned back in his chair. "What do you tell them?" he asked.

"I tell them straight. I tell them you're the toughest one we've ever had."

"I bet you don't say it that way," he responded.

"I do say it that way," I said. "But I follow it up by saying that off the field, you're one of the finest individuals I've ever been around: a great father, and a great person, and somebody I have the utmost respect for."

"Well, General Burleson, I appreciate that, and I hope you know I don't mean any of those things I say on the field. I just get caught up in the heat of the moment, and my adrenaline gets going, and I sometimes lose control."

"I know what you're saying," I said. "The problem is that 85,000 fans in the stands and millions of television viewers think you mean it."

Arkansas: Houston Nutt (1998-Present)

Arkansas hasn't been in the conference very long so I didn't have many coaches to choose from. I mentioned Coach Danny Ford in other parts of the book, and this is meant as no slight to him. He was a very good coach and has done well at several schools. He was unusual in that he was about as calm and loose before a game as any coach I've ever known, at least outwardly. I remember one time when I walked into the dressing room for a pregame meeting and John Daly, the professional golfer, was in there with him giving him some golf tips.

The reason I picked Coach Nutt was because in my opinion he conducts himself the way an official would really like a coach to. On the field he keeps a level of poise and dignity that is rare in the coaching profession. On the other hand, he is also one of the most competitive coaches I have ever been around. He was a successful college athlete in several sports, and that drive shows in his personality. He doesn't let it take over though; he never loses control of himself on the field. You've heard coaches referred to as "players' coaches." Well Houston Nutt is an official's coach.

Auburn: Pat Dye (1981-1992)

I worked with several coaches at Auburn, but by far the most memorable was Coach Pat Dye. When he came into the league, I had been there a few years and was a somewhat established official. The prime of my career coincided with the prime of his, and not surprisingly I worked a lot of his games. One thing I noticed about him was his transformation over time. When I came into the league he was very critical of officials and extremely vocal about things. As time went on though, he became one of the senior statesmen of the league and handled them in a different way. It wasn't that he didn't get as upset; he just showed it in a more subtle manner.

Another thing about him that I have to mention is that of all the coaches I worked for, Coach Dye was as completely in charge in his practices of anybody. He did a great job delegating, but there was never a question as to who the boss was.

But the things I appreciate most about Coach Dye are that he never held a grudge and wasn't superstitious. For some strange reason, I was involved in a lot of his games that were decided by controversial calls during the first few years he was at Auburn, and most of the calls went against him. To my knowledge, none were calls I made—I just happened to be the one who relayed them to everyone. I have a great appreciation for him because I know that had I been in his situation, I would have looked at Dick Burleson and said, "Well maybe he's a good official, but I have a bad-luck streak going with him, and I don't know if I want him working my games." Yet I was never struck from his games, and I will always have a deep appreciation for Coach Dye for not giving up on me early in his career.

Florida: Steve Spurrier (1990-2001)

This was an easy one. Coach Spurrier has been the most recognizable coach in the Southeastern Conference since Coach Bryant at Alabama. I do, however, have to give an honorable mention to Coach Charley Pell. I do that because I had such a long history with him. He was from Albertville, which was near my hometown of Blountsville. We grew up around the same time so we knew each other through sports, mutual friends, and such. We got reacquainted later on when he was coaching Jacksonville State and I was officiating in the Gulf South Conference. He left and went to Clemson about the same time I moved up into the SEC, and he followed me to the SEC soon thereafter. We always had a great relationship, and I was sorry to see him leave the way he did.

Coach Pell woke me up one Saturday morning during the first fall he was coaching at Florida. "Dick? Charley Pell," he said.

"Yeah, good morning, Coach. How ya doing?"

"Can you get down here to Gainesville a week from today and work my early scrimmage?"

"Well yeah, I suppose I could do that."

"Good," he said, "because I need somebody down here who can talk to my team about the rules, but I really want you down here to talk to my team about sportsmanship. I want the University of Florida football players to know the relationship that an official has with players like those from the University of Alabama. I want you to talk about class, I want you to talk about professionalism, I want them to hear what it's like for a team that is rarely penalized, and why. I just want them to know that side of an official-player relationship. You don't even have to talk about new rules or anything, but I want you to talk about that."

So I did that for him, and I always look back on that as a good way to get started at a new program. I always had a lot of respect for him.

As for the most memorable coach, what can I say about Coach Spurrier that hasn't already been said? What can you say about a man who shows up out of nowhere, disappears just as quickly 12 years later, and turns one of the stodgiest old conferences on edge during that time? He changed everything and made sure everyone knew it. He is one of a kind.

In my radio appearances and speaking engagements, I get a lot of questions about Coach Spurrier. People see him throwing the visor, pitching a fit, making enemy after enemy at press conferences, and they just know he has to be one of the most difficult to work for of all the coaches around. I always tell them I hate to disappoint them, but from an official's point of view, Coach Spurrier was one of the best coaches around.

People are almost always taken aback by this revelation. They can't believe I would say something like that. It's true though. Most all of the visor-throwing and temper tantrums were aimed at his own players, mainly his quarterbacks. He actually handled officials well on the sideline; he would grit his teeth and grimace and throw the occasional visor, but he usually wouldn't get onto the officials during a game. The only thing that was tough about him from an officiating standpoint was that he never forgot a bad call.

I don't mean this lightly, either. If you made a bad call or just something he perceived to be a bad call, he would always remember it. If the opportunity presented itself, he would remind you of a call you made seven years earlier.

Another thing I remember about him was that I never met a coach who was more focused when I met with him in the dressing room before the game. He knew what he wanted to do and had his whole game plan memorized. He also knew his opponent from every standpoint, to the point where he would remind you that their left offensive tackle held on every third down and things like that. He was a master at it.

I worked a lot of his Georgia-Florida games. One that particularly stands out was the 1994 game. The game was usually played at the Gator Bowl in Jacksonville, but during renovations to that stadium, it became a home-and-home series. I worked the one in Gainesville. It felt strange to be working a Georgia-Florida game at Florida Field.

There had been thunderstorms brewing all day on the day of the game, and about a half-hour before game time the clouds opened up and a torrential storm hit out of nowhere. It was a bad scene. There was thunder and lightning all around, people were running for cover, and the players broke out of their warm-ups and took off for the locker rooms. It was a nationally televised game, and I wasn't sure exactly what to do to get it back on schedule.

I went back to the officials' dressing room and called the National Weather Service to see what they could tell me. Somehow I got through on the first try and got a live person on the other end instead of a recording. "Sir, my name is Dick Burleson, and I'm the head referee for the Georgia-Florida game." I told him. "I'm wondering if you could tell me anything about this storm so I can tell the television people and the coaches what we're going to do."

"Well, Mr. Burleson, I'll tell you," he said. "I've been tracking this storm for a while, and it's coming across really fast. If you will wait exactly 15 minutes, this storm will be over, and in 16 minutes you'll have a clear sky for the rest of the game."

"Are you sure about that?" I asked him.

"I'm absolutely positive," he said.

So I came out of my dressing room, and Coach Spurrier and Coach Ray Goff of Georgia are right outside my door wanting to know what's going on. "I'll tell you what we're going to do," I said. "We're going to wait 15 minutes, and the storm is going to end. In 16 minutes the stars will be out."

They looked at me as if I were crazy. I didn't tell them anything more, and sure enough, everything I said came true exactly like I had been told.

The last thing I want to say about Coach Spurrier concerns his headwear. He was known as "The Visor" by many people, for obvious reasons. I was talking to him in a dressing room one day and told him that my wife, Mary, wore a visor when she played tennis. I told him she had commented on how he had showed up one day without one, and she had wondered where his visor was. This was on a Saturday. The following Tuesday, a package arrived in the mail from Gainesville. Inside was one of Steve Spurrier's visors, which he had signed for Mary.

Georgia: Vince Dooley (1964-1988)

For some reason, I worked significantly more University of Georgia games than any other school during my 25 years in the SEC. Through that, I got to know Coach Dooley very well. As an official, one of the cardinal sins is to pick favorites, but I figure since I'm no longer on the field, it's okay. I get asked the question a lot, and if I had to choose, I'd have to say he was my favorite coach. My reasoning is that even though I worked more games for him, I never had one minute of trouble from him.

I think one of the reasons we got along so well was that he was a military historian, and I always thought he would have had a great aptitude for military leadership. He was calm on the outside but very much in charge and extremely competitive. On top of that, he was a consummate gentleman. He was just a pleasure to be around. Only one time did he ever get really mad at me; just once in all the years I worked for him.

They were playing Clemson, and that has always been a fierce rivalry. Right at the end of the first half, Georgia recovered a Clemson fumble deep in Clemson territory. There were maybe 20 seconds left before halftime. They had time to make a couple of plays and then try for a field goal.

So we signaled that it was Georgia's ball, and everybody went nuts on the field. The game was in Athens, so the crowd was going berserk. In the confusion, one of the Georgia players ran up to me and said he wanted a timeout. They had one left, so that was okay, but the problem was that the clock was stopped anyway on the change of possession so there was no need for it. But there was no question; it wasn't a quick thing that he took back. He was in our face yelling "timeout." We had no choice but to grant him the final, useless timeout of the half.

As soon as he found this out, Coach Dooley absolutely went into orbit. The genteel exterior vanished, and he just went crazy. He asked me and the other official who was near me who had called the timeout. Problem was, we didn't know—we had been focusing on other things and simply didn't remember. This made it worse as the assistant coaches started to pick up on it and began insisting that Georgia had not called timeout and that we made a mistake. We insisted that they had called it and stood our ground.

As it turned out, Georgia was held out of the end zone on that drive, and Coach Dooley was still very upset with me, which as I said was completely out of character for him. I didn't know what to tell him. I still couldn't identify the player—I just knew absolutely that somebody had called timeout. We left the field in a shower of boos.

Now at Sanford Stadium all the dressing rooms are right together, and everyone goes in and out through the same walkway. I was in the dressing room with my crew, and I tried to muster some damage control and figure out which player had called that timeout. Nobody knew, but everyone backed me up because they heard the guy say it.

So we came back on the field to start the second half, and Coach Dooley walks straight over to me. The crowd picks up on it and starts booing again. "I just want to apologize for that scene right before the half," he said.

"I understand, Coach, I know how things get," I replied.

"No, what you don't understand is that the player who called timeout confessed to me in the locker room. I was wrong, and I wanted to let you know that." Knowing Coach Dooley, I think he would have apologized even if the player hadn't confessed.

Kentucky: Bill Curry (1990-1996)

I picked Coach Bill Curry because he was as tough a competitor as anyone I've ever seen but always had a lot of class. It was my impression that he brought class to any program he coached. Not to say he wouldn't get mad sometimes, but he always kept things in perspective and never got carried away with it.

I think one reason I always had a great relationship with Coach Curry was that he was a Georgia Tech man, and so we had something in common right off the bat. He started there the year after I graduated so we were never there together and never knew each other. We missed each other by three months, and therefore I was not restricted from working his games. In practices and pregame meetings we would share our favorite Tech stories.

One game that stands out was when Kentucky played Indiana at Bloomington in September 1995. It was a treat to be able to go out of conference to a place I generally would not visit. It was a great experience; they put us in rooms in the student union center, and Coach Bobby Knight came down and had breakfast with us on game day. He was quite a character, to say the least.

In the dressing room before the game, we went through our regular meeting rituals. I wished him good luck and turned to leave. He stopped me. "Dick, did you ever have Professor Vail for math when you were at Tech?" he asked.

"As a matter of fact I did," I said. Professor Vail was an icon at Georgia Tech. Everyone knew him, and everyone who had him for a class wanted to talk about him. So while everyone else stood around looking confused, we went off talking about a math professor we'd had 30 years before.

A vivid scene stands out in my mind about Coach Curry, and I think it says a lot about him as a coach and his respect for tradition. It was during his time at Alabama, when I was working a scrimmage for him. He was pretty laid-back that day, as he usually was. As it was a regular game-type scrimmage, he was on the sideline instead of standing on the field like coaches do a lot of the time.

At one point in the scrimmage, a receiver caught the ball, and a cornerback came out of nowhere and absolutely nailed him. This wasn't an everyday hit either; it took the receiver a couple of minutes to regain his senses. While he was on the ground recuperating, the defensive back proceeded to stand over him and showboat, pointing and taunting him.

I was getting things ready for the next play, when I felt something coming up behind me. Before I could turn around, it whizzed past me—it was Coach Curry making a beeline for the cornerback. I thought at first he was going to congratulate him for making a great play because it was the highlight of the scrimmage. He grabbed the player and shook him until I thought he was going to shake his head off and yelled right in his face, "Don't you ever do that as long as you wear a crimson jersey!" he screamed. "I don't want to see you do that in practice, in a scrimmage, or especially in a game." He got that young man's attention, as well as the rest of the team's. You could have heard a pin drop on that field at that time. I know he got my attention; I didn't blow the whistle for the next play until he got through. He let them know that was unacceptable at the University of Alabama and would not happen under his watch.

LSU: Charlie McClendon (1962-1979)

There were a lot of coaches at LSU during my 25 years, and people might ask me why I'd pick Coach McClendon. It was a difficult decision since I have always had tremendous respect for Coach Mike Archer, Coach Bill Arnsparger, and Coach Gerry DiNardo. They were all class people, and I had memorable games with each of them.

Coach McClendon was not only a great coach but also a class act. He had a great sense of humor, and I enjoyed working with him. At the first SEC meeting I ever attended with all the officials and coaches, Coach McClendon stood up and explained how we were all missing his reverse handoff on LSU kickoffs. We were ruling forward, and he said it was backward. Before we could say anything, Coach Bryant's growling voice came from the back of the room: "Sit down and shut up, Charley Mac—you shouldn't be running that stupid play anyway!" Coach McClendon quickly and quietly took his seat.

Ole Miss: Tommy Tuberville (1995-1997)

Much like LSU, there were a lot of coaches at Ole Miss during my tenure in the SEC. There were some very good ones too. In the category of "most memorable" however, I have to go with Coach Tuberville. I pick him mainly because of his personality. Though he can get as excited as anybody on the field, he was always personable and had a good relationship with the officials. I always felt like Coach Tuberville handled things the right way.

He's also very good with his fans. I have a friend who is a rabid Rebel fan, and I took him to a scrimmage one day. He had been bugging me about meeting the coaches for a while, so I obliged and brought him with me. I told him to stay on the sideline and stay out of the way, and if there was an opportunity, I'd introduce him to Coach Tuberville and whoever else was around. So after the scrimmage was over, I took my friend to Coach Tuberville's office and introduced them. I figured it would be a handshake, a "nice to meet you," and we would be on our way. As it turned out, Coach Tuberville invited my friend to sit with him in his office and talk football, and he talked to him until I came back and broke them up because I was afraid he was taking too much of the coach's time. That definitely told me something about how he ran his program and the relationships he established with people. I would imagine that as a recruit it would be hard to say no to him. People say he's a tremendous salesman, and he's certainly got the personality for it.

Mississippi State: Jackie Sherrill (1991-2003)

Another difficult choice. For some strange reason, I never met a Mississippi State person I didn't like. Believe me, I've looked for them, just to see if there's a rotten one out there, but to no avail. That may change tomorrow, but as far as I can tell, they just seem to be all-around great people. A classic example is friend Marvin Ratcliff. Coach Emory Ballard was one of my all-time favorite coaches; I had a tremendous amount of respect for him. The same goes for Coach Rocky Felker. Coach Felker was one of the most beloved Mississippi State people who ever existed. But as far as memorable coaches, Jackie Sherrill is it.

Coach Sherrill was tough to work for. He's an outstanding coach, as his record will back up, and he expects the same degree of effort put in to officiating that he puts into coaching. There's nothing wrong with that by any means; we all do the same. But he's tough. He's not as vocal as he once was—he took on the role of one of the elder statesmen of the league and wasn't quite as active as in his earlier days. He places a lot of emphasis on seniority and respect. He had a lot more patience with a call if it was made by one of the senior officials than he did with a younger official, one who hasn't earned the same amount of respect over the years.

This isn't unusual. It takes a while to earn the respect of coaches. By the time they make it to the SEC, head coaches have been around the game for years. They feel uneasy trusting their life's work to a youngster; they are much more comfortable when they see some gray hair.

South Carolina: Brad Scott (1994-1998)

Like Arkansas, South Carolina hasn't been in the Southeastern Conference very long so I haven't had experience with too many coaches. I chose Coach Scott because apart from being very much a gentleman, he could hold his own against any referee in his knowledge of the rules.

There's a difference between knowing the rules and being what I call "rules knowledgeable." If Coach Scott challenged you on a rule, you were well advised to listen to what he had to say because he was probably right. He didn't make a big fuss, though. He was quiet and reserved, and we rarely had any trouble out of him, but you always knew he was watching you closely.

While I'm on the subject of South Carolina, I have to say a little bit about their fans. My first experience with them was a game against Georgia in Athens. It's a pretty big rivalry, a great border war, and the Gamecock fans were there in droves. I was checking into the Ramada Inn the night before the game when I saw a bus full of South Carolinians pull up into the parking lot. I figured it'd be a noisy night, but I didn't think much of it until I saw them open the luggage compartment under the bus. There was no luggage in the luggage compartment. There was no room for luggage as the entire thing was filled to capacity with beer. These people were hard-core. My suspicions were correct; it was a very loud night at the hotel as their rooms were directly above mine.

Another thing I noticed about their fans is how vocal they are. As you probably already could figure out, the crowd noise rule is written to be used against the home team to protect visiting players from overzealous crowds. It was never intended to be used on a visiting squad. Nevertheless, at this game at Sanford Stadium, South Carolina Gamecock fans had bought every ticket they could get their hands on. They took up an entire end zone, all the way out to about the 10-yard-line on both sides of the field. They made so much noise at that end of the field that the Georgia quarterback could not hear the signals. I thought I was going to have an embarrassing situation on my hands where I had to invoke the crowd noise rule against the visiting fans. That says something about how devoted South Carolina fans are. Those people are road warriors.

Tennessee: Johnny Majors (1977-1992)

I had many years with Coach Majors, and much like Coach Pat Dye at Auburn, his prime time was my prime time. I have to mention Coach Philip Fulmer as well, if nothing else to say that officiating for him was a pleasure. He always treats the officials well, and I have no complaints about him from an officiating standpoint. I picked Coach Majors mainly because of the many years I worked with him—after working with someone for so long, you tend to establish a professional closeness with them, and I had that with Coach Majors.

The thing that I always think of about Coach Majors was that he was always the same—before the game, on the sideline, in practice, whenever. He was always a gentleman, never got out of line, even at his most heated moments. He was also extremely organized. He had a routine he went through before every game. As soon as I came into the dressing room before the game, he would take me over to a chalkboard where he had everything he wanted to talk to me about written down. He would methodically go down the list, explaining everything in detail. He usually had some sort of trick play to make sure we knew about, as well as anything he had noticed about the other team that we needed to take note of.

As long as I worked for him, Coach Majors was not a complainer. The league office would never hear about anything he didn't agree with or disapproved of. He was universally one of the good guys in football.

One other thing I have to mention about the University of Tennessee, and this isn't restricted to them: Their entire athletic department goes out of their way to make sure the officials are taken care of and treated well before and during the game. Most teams do that as well, but no other school works harder to take care of the officials than Tennessee does. They had a man named Gus Manning who worked as a liaison for the officials and made sure everything was the way it should be.

Vanderbilt: Watson Brown (1986-1990)

I worked for eight different Vanderbilt coaches during my 25 years. Some were really good, even though most lacked success at Vandy. I picked Coach Brown for a couple of reasons. First of all, I always felt he was the perfect fit for Vanderbilt. He was a hero there as a player, he loved the university, and he had a great football mind. A lot of people refer to him as an "offensive genius," and I can't say that I disagree.

People have a tendency to associate calmness and gentlemanly behavior with a lack of a competitive spirit. There are few tougher competitors than Coach Brown. I've seen him absolutely tear an official's ear off when he thought he made a bad call. But he keeps it professional and leaves his emotions on the field.

I also have to add that I have a personal reason for picking Coach Brown, and that is because he was my neighbor for several years. He moved into my neighborhood when he was hired to coach at UAB, and I got to know him on a personal level, outside of football. I can say he's every bit the gentleman away from the game as he is on the field.

Chapter 7

Other Great Personalities

I have been fortunate during my years in the Southeastern Conference to have worked with three great league commissioners. When I started in 1972, the commissioner was Dr. Boyd McWhorter, followed in 1986 by Dr. Harvey Schiller and in 1990 by Roy Kramer. They were very different people, each with their own distinct management style and concept, and that made them all unique to work with. Their personalities were wildly disparate, but they all worked closely with the football officials because they understood the importance of football to the conference. They knew what was at stake each Saturday and the pressure we were under every time we went on the field, and they appreciated that. I recently have had the opportunity to work with the new commissioner, Mike Slive, and I am very impressed. I have full faith that he will uphold the tradition in the SEC.

The one common thread that bound the commissioners together was their unwavering commitment to the integrity of conference officiating. They all maintained that if the integrity of college football officiating was ever compromised, the game as we know it would be finished. The fans would lose confidence in the sport, and it would be reduced to a joke. They went to great lengths to make sure nothing interfered with our doing the best job we could. They were well aware of the abundance of gambling in college football and did everything they could to shield us from it. At the beginning of every season they would bring in representatives from the FBI to talk with us about gamblers, what to watch for, and what to do in case we were approached by one.

When I was originally brought into the SEC to officiate in 1972, the supervisor of officials was a man named George Gardner. He was widely known as the father of SEC officiating, having started the first association of officials and led it from its inception in 1945 until 1973. He was succeeded by Mr. Cliff Harper, who held the position until 1980 and who was a tremendous influence on my life and my officiating career. After him, for one season, Hootie Ingram was supervisor; he would go on to be the Athletic Director at Alabama. Gordon Pettus, a great SEC official and another of my biggest influences, took his place in 1982 and held the position until 1988. Since 1989 Bobby Gaston has served in the supervisor role. He was also a great football official I had the pleasure of working with on several occasions. Another person who has been invaluable to SEC officials has been Executive Associate Commissioner Mark Womack; he has always been on our side, supporting and standing behind the officials even during times when it was not popular to do so.

These men all echoed the sentiments of the commissioners with whom I have worked that the integrity of officiating is of utmost importance and is something to be protected above all else. I dare say it meant even more to them than to the commissioners since they were closer to the action. If the quality of SEC officiating were to falter, the supervisor of officials would be the first person blamed.

And while talking about the SEC, I absolutely have to mention the four football officiating secretaries who worked at the league office since I have been there. They are the glue that holds the whole thing together. They are responsible for travel arrangements, substituting officials as needed, and dealing with and fixing any last-minute problems that come up. I couldn't forgive myself if I neglected to include them.

When I first came into the league, a lady named Loretta Wallace had this unenviable job. She was followed by Carrol Lowry Crocker, who wrote a history of officiating in the Southeastern Conference that was indispensable in the writing of this book. Kathryn Poe-Switzer was another secretary of officials who is now the administrative assistant to the commissioner, and she was succeeded by Megan Patterson, who remains in the position. They have all done a great job, for without them everything relating to officials in the SEC would be chaos.

Being a Southeastern Conference official for so many years, I had the opportunity to meet and work with people of great influence and fame. At the risk of namedropping, I'd like to mention some of them.

Keith Jackson

One of the greatest thrills I ever had as an official was the opportunity to meet and work with Keith Jackson. To me, and to most fans of the game, his is the voice of college football. He was the announcer for several of my games, and it was a treat every time I was fortunate enough to work with him. One thing I have always admired about him is how he acts as a calming voice on controversial calls. He was never one to jump to conclusions or to get on to an official over a close call. It's not that he is never critical of a call, if there's a mistake he says so, but he does it in a way so as not to embarrass the official or make him look bad. That speaks a lot of the respect he has for the game. He and Bob Griese were the announcers for my last game, and I'll get to that in a later chapter.

Bob Neal

Another great announcer I had the pleasure of working with was Bob Neal. He did the SEC Game of the Week when it first started and has since moved on to NBA basketball games. His son Dave is the announcer for Jefferson-Pilot games now. He was a class act all around. One thing he always did that I admired was to meet with the supervisor of officials before every season to go over new rules and make sure he was on top of any changes for that season. His main reason was so that he could avoid unfairly criticizing someone for a call that was actually correct. This was not always standard practice for football announcers. This is why he'll always be one of my favorites.

John Ferguson

Radio announcers have a different relationship with officials than do television announcers. Almost all teams have their own radio personalities who go with them to every game. Television is different—television announcers are provided by the network or whoever is broadcasting the game. Because of this, officials get to know them fairly well over time.

Not that I could choose a single one, but one of my favorite radio personalities has always been John Ferguson, who announced for LSU for many years. I always felt he did a masterful job of painting a picture for the listener without using too many words. My dad used to listen to his broadcasts whenever I would be officiating an LSU game, and he said he only had two words for a pass: complete and incomplete. He didn't fool around with extra description; he told you exactly what happened first. If something interesting happened, then he would tell about it, but he was all about business first. He did it with class too. He gave criticism where it was due but not where it wasn't—that's all you can really ask for out of a radio announcer. He was a classic.

General Colin Powell

One of the greatest people I've ever known, and one who had little to do with football, was General Colin Powell. As Commanding General of all the Army Reserve forces in the Southeast, I got to host him when he came through the South in March 1993, which was during his tenure as Chairman of the Joint Chiefs of Staff.

I don't know what I thought of him before, whether I had any opinion or not, but after spending the day with General Colin Powell, I am convinced that there is no finer human being on earth. I have never before or since met a person who could command that level of respect in such a short time.

Alabama had won the national championship the previous year, and when they found out that General Powell was going to be in Birmingham, they wanted him to come address the team in Tuscaloosa. One of my fellow generals was a member of an Alabama booster club and asked me if they could borrow him for part of the day. I told him I didn't know if General Powell would be receptive to that, but I would ask. I was nervous enough with him coming to my headquarters to present some awards and wasn't sure exactly how to ask. As it turned out, he was very gracious and loved the idea of meeting the team.

As we were driving to the presentation from the airport, General Powell made sure he was clear on our agenda. "So I see we're going to Tuscaloosa this afternoon," he said.

"Yes, Sir," I said. "Coach Stallings is down there, and he wants you to address the University of Alabama national championship football team."

"Well I'm really looking forward to it. This should be a lot of fun," he said.

Part of his visit included a short speech at the Galleria Mall, and we had a Blackhawk helicopter sitting in the parking lot to take him to Tuscaloosa. The plan was to land on the practice field right next to the football offices. As it happened however, General Powell's visit coincided with one of the worst snowstorms the state of Alabama had ever had. It was so bad that the Blackhawk was unable to take off.

We figured we would just have to scrub the trip since we couldn't use the helicopter and we were all the way across town from the airport. We talked to General Powell about it, but he was adamant about making it to Tuscaloosa. "No problem," he said. "We'll just drive down there. We already have the state troopers with us— we'll have them lead the way."

It was a good idea. The only problem was that his plane was at the Birmingham airport. "What about your plane?" I asked.

"We'll just get them to fly it down to Tuscaloosa and take me back to Washington from there."

So we did. He finished the speech at the Galleria, and we drove off to Tuscaloosa. Now the storm was coming in from the west so as we drove, we were heading into it. By the time we got down there, it was snowing so bad we could hardly see.

When we finally got to the football complex, the house was packed. People were practically hanging from the rafters in the media room. Players, coaches, trainers, secretaries, students—everyone wanted to see General Colin Powell. He made his speech and, not surprisingly, brought the house down.

I had told Coach Stallings before everything had happened that General Powell wasn't allowed to accept gifts of any significant value as an active Army general, so I asked him not to embarrass everybody by giving him something he has to give right back. He said he understood and would keep that in mind.

The first thing they did after the speech was to give him a football signed by the whole team. That was no problem. Then they brought out an Alabama jersey with "Powell" on the back and the number 1. I'm watching everything from the front row and at one point Coach Stallings looks down at me with a grin and says, "Now, General Burleson said we couldn't give you anything of any value. I just want you to know we don't pay a lot for our footballs and our jerseys."

So that got him off the hook a bit, but then he followed it up. "General Powell," he said, "I had a lot of stuff I wanted to give you—running shoes, warm-ups, all sorts of great stuff I was going to give you today, but again, General Burleson said I couldn't give it to you because of regulations."

I looked behind Coach Stallings and saw a large box full of different things. "Now, in this box is all the stuff I was planning to give to you. But as it turns out, I can't. However, I know you're going to retire in about three months, and the day you retire, this box will be on your front doorstep." And I'm sure it was.

We had a great time visiting the facilities, and General Powell loved every minute of it. Finally the Air Force captain came and told me that the weather was getting to the point that soon the plane wouldn't be able to take off. He told me I needed to break them up soon since there was no de-icing equipment on the plane and they were close to being snowed in. So I reluctantly relayed the news, and we got General Powell out of there and back to Washington. I just want to reiterate though, that my entire time with him was a pleasure and that there have been few people with whom I have spent that little time but who have had as much of an effect on me as General Colin Powell.

SEC Football Fans—The BEST!

I've said this several times on radio shows and in speeches, but we have the best of all worlds in the Southeastern Conference. This comes from somebody who has worked with other conferences and has been around a good bit. We have the best players, schools, coaches, officials (though I may be a bit biased), and above all, the best fans.

The SEC has the most knowledgeable football fans anywhere. They're rabid, too. They don't hesitate to let an official know when they disagree with a call. The thing is that they generally know what they're talking (or yelling) about. I am a frequent guest on the Paul Finebaum show in Birmingham, and one of the things I do on the show is talk to callers. It's amazing how well they know their football, right down to the smallest detail. Sometimes I'll be listening to the show and someone will have some obscure question that they can't figure out, and I'll be tempted to call in and explain it to them, but usually before I can dial, someone else has called and straightened them out.

They're a great group. I consider myself very lucky to have had the opportunity to work in the SEC, the best conference in football.

As I said before, I consider SEC fans to be the best college football fans anywhere. In general, they are the most knowledgeable, passionate, and respectful fans I have had the pleasure to be around. However, they do have a tendency to go a bit overboard on occasion.

Earlier in the book, you'll find the story about the LSU-Florida game where I added time to the clock after it had run out and Florida ended up winning. After that game, I got the one and only letter a fan ever sent me. An LSU fan got my address somehow. At the time our hometowns were listed with our names in game programs. (Fortunately this doesn't happen anymore.) I guess he found a Birmingham telephone book and located my address.

The letter showed up in my mailbox the week after the game. The postmark on the letter was from somewhere in Louisiana—I don't recall where. It was a well-written letter, obviously composed by an intelligent person. He even signed his name as I recall. The letter read:

Dear Mr. Burleson;

I have watched you officiate LSU football games for years. I always considered you one of the very best. However, after cheating us out of the ball game Saturday night, I am very upset with you, and I feel like you were solely responsible for that call. If you value your life, you will never set foot in Tiger Stadium again.

The FBI used to talk with all SEC officials every year, instructing us on what to do if we were approached by gamblers. They touch on other subjects, such as what to do about threatening fans, as well. Anything of this nature was to be turned over to the FBI. I thought about that, but I didn't share it with anybody at the time. I came to the conclusion that this fellow couldn't say all those nice things at the beginning without being a rational person who was simply caught up in the moment. So I didn't take it too seriously.

The unfortunate epilogue to this story was that 10 days later I had my next game in Tiger Stadium. I knew this already, and as much as I tried not to let that thought get to me, I'd be lying if I said it didn't creep into my head a few times. Nothing came of it, but you can be sure I was on the alert for any suspicious activity the next time I found myself in Baton Rouge. Perhaps surprisingly that was the only threatening letter I ever received in 25 years of officiating in the SEC.

Chapter 8

Great SEC Football Rivalries

As an SEC official, I had the privilege to work some of the greatest rivalries in any sport anywhere. Those games were always special to me, I always felt like I was taking part in something that was of greater importance than just any normal football game.

Auburn-Georgia

The Auburn-Georgia game is the oldest rivalry in the SEC. The game was always a border war, and the 1980s were the best time for it. Both teams had coaches who had played for the other school, Georgia's coach Vince Dooley went to Auburn, and Pat Dye, Auburn's coach, went to Georgia. Also, both teams were top 25 contenders every year, and their game went a long way toward determining the SEC champion of the year.

The rivalry between the two schools was and is an intense one. Even before I started officiating, when the game was played at Columbus, Georgia, every year, I remember hearing horror stories of giant brawls between the two factions. I worked my share of those games, and fortunately there were few altercations on my watch.

Auburn-Tennessee

Auburn-Tennessee was always a great game, and it provided me with some great memories. I worked several of them, but one of my favorite stories was one told to me by my friend Pete Williams, about something that happened in a game I did not work. It was during Bo Jackson's tenure at Auburn.

I talked about this in an earlier chapter, but just to recap, the umpire is essentially the "middle linebacker" of the officiating crew. He stands behind the defensive line and watches that part of the field. There's an unwritten rule that when he's standing there and the running back charges through the line, the umpire freezes in place so as not to interfere with the play. This is important because he doesn't know which way the running back will go, and if he moves, chances are the running back will go that way as well. So the tacit agreement is that the umpire freezes and the running back does not run over him. This rule also works because if the running back is alert, he can use the umpire as a sort of makeshift blocker, running to the opposite side from any would-be tacklers.

Generally Bo Jackson was one of the best at using the umpire as a blocker. He had an instinct that told him which way to run to avoid defenders that was rarely wrong. On one play in the Auburn-Tennessee game, he must have had something distracting him because he didn't quite follow the agreement. He came charging through the line like always and Pete froze in place, as he was supposed to do. The difference on this play was that instead of altering his course accordingly, Bo Jackson simply plowed over poor Pete. Bo made it to the end zone relatively easily; meanwhile Pete lay on the ground with three broken ribs. As they carried Pete off the field, he wheezed, "Did I stop him?"

Auburn had a great football team in 1989. They would end the season 10-2 with a share of the SEC championship. They came to Knoxville ranked fourth in the AP poll and on their way to a very successful season. Tennessee was having a respectable year as well, ranked 14th in the AP poll. None of this mattered though, as the crowd would have more to say about the outcome of this game than the players.

It's late in the fourth quarter, and Tennessee is up by a touchdown, 21-14. Tennessee has the ball and wants to run out the clock. They are on about their own 30-yard line, and it's fourth down. The clock starts running down, gets below 10 seconds, and the crowd starts counting along with it. Auburn has a timeout left, so they call it and stop the clock. The Tennessee fans continue counting however, and when they reach zero (remember the clock is stopped at eight), the place goes berserk. In their collective mind, Tennessee has just knocked off the number 4 team in the nation. They swarm the field, probably 25,000 of them, and I don't know what to do. The game is not over, but I have no idea how to get these people off the field, and I'm starting to worry for our own safety.

The next thing I know, a goalpost comes down and is broken into pieces, which are then carried through the crowd. The crowd turns their eyes on the other goalpost and begin to tear it down as well. I go over to Pat Dye, Auburn's coach, who is understandably an unhappy camper.

"Coach, you can see what a mess we have here, but if you want to play the final seven seconds of the game, we will clear the field, and we will play the final seconds. It's up to you," I tell him.

He doesn't say a word, just looks at the chaos swirling around him. I turn around to walk off and try to clear the field. The next thing I know, a tremendous roar goes up from the stands. I look around, and Coach Dye is leading his team across the field to shake hands with Coach Majors and signal the end of the game.

From a safety standpoint, this was the best thing he could have done. There were thousands of Tennessee fans flooding the playing surface, pieces of goalpost were flying around—it was everything short of a full-scale riot. Coach Dye demonstrated a great deal of wisdom by letting things lie as they were.

Georgia-Florida

Known affectionately as "the world's largest cocktail party," Georgia versus Florida is a special game. Apart from a two-year period where it was played on the respective campuses, the game is played in Jacksonville, Florida, with the tickets split equally between the two teams. This creates a wonderful atmosphere for football, and it's always an enjoyable game to officiate. Something notable almost always happens as well.

My first Georgia-Florida game gets off to a dubious start. On the third play from scrimmage, the Georgia running back bowls over the head linesman, knocking him over and breaking his leg. In the SEC, we prepare for this by bringing an extra official to run the clock. In the event something like this happens, we either run one official short or we get the spare official to abandon his clock-operating duties and come on the field to replace the injured official. We decide to run the rest of the game one official short so we can keep the scoreboard clock running.

Right at the beginning of the second half, a Florida receiver runs a crossing route and hits my back judge at full speed, knocking him out of the game. Now I'm two officials short, and I have a couple of dilemmas. First, I have to run one official short and without a scoreboard clock, which could potentially create complete havoc on the field. Second, I have to go over to my clock-operator, who has just watched two of his colleagues sustain fairly severe injuries, and tell him I need him on the field in the line of fire. He gripped the control tightly, not wanting to leave the sideline.

The 1993 Georgia-Florida game is turning out to be one of the best games I've ever worked. Florida is on their way to a 10-2 season and an SEC championship, while Georgia is struggling to a 5-6 record. The fourth quarter is coming to a close, and somehow Georgia has managed to keep it close so far. All they need is a touchdown and an extra point to tie the game.

Georgia's quarterback is Eric Zeier, who would go on to finish in the top 10 in the Heisman Trophy balloting two years in a row. He has played a great game and is leading the Bulldogs down the field toward the possible game-winning touchdown.

Georgia has the ball deep in Florida territory with time for one more play.

The teams line up, and Zeier drops back to pass. He finds a receiver open in the end zone and hits him with a perfect strike. The red and black side of the Gator Bowl goes crazy, thinking they might have the game won—or at least tied.

There is one problem however. Just prior to the snap, a Florida defensive back noticed something he didn't like and called timeout. This was one of the few times the instant replay actually helped officials. Nobody heard a whistle before the snap, but one of the officials in my crew is adamant that he was signaling while the ball was still set, rendering the ball dead and nullifying the play.

There was no use of instant replay in college football at the time so we couldn't look to it for help, but later on the television replay you could see the Florida player clearly signaling and the official's hands moving upward to signal timeout well before the ball is snapped. The timeout is over, and the teams line up to run the final play of the game again. The play is similar to the one that was nullified, except for one crucial detail: a Florida player knocks the pass down and it falls incomplete. Florida wins.

A photograph of the final play of the game was on the front of newspaper sports sections across the country. A photograph of Eric Zeier with his head on the ground in despair and me above him signaling "no good" after the pass went incomplete is in this book (see page 110).

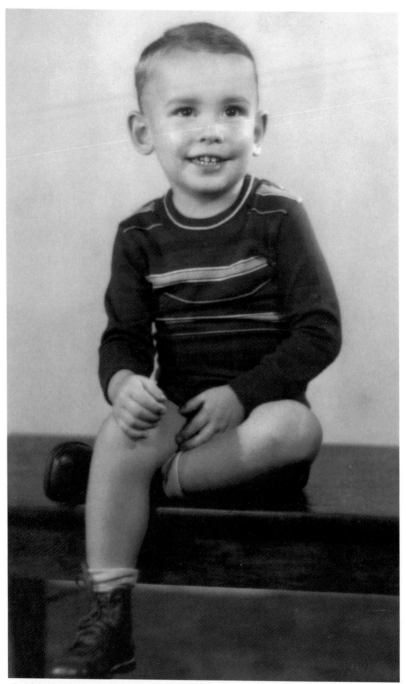

Evidently Dick liked stripes at an early age.

Dick with his high-school sweetheart, Mary, at the Blount County Fair after a game

(Front row, center) Dick Burleson, cocaptain and All-County 1956-57, J.B. Pennington High School (Blountsville, Alabama) basketball team.

Dickie Burleson, Center

Dick Burleson, a four-year letterman at J.B. Pennington High School (Blountsville, Alabama), earned All-State recognition as center and linebacker.

SENIORS — 1956

Front row, l. to r.: Asst. Coach Bill Driskell, Kenneth Brown, Prentice Hicks, Travis Hunt, Joe Brindley, Larry House, Coach E. L. Starkey. Back row: Charlie Chamblee, Waylon Thrasher, Wilburn Wynn, Kyle Absher, Richard Burleson, John Bellenger. Not shown: James Brindley, Frank Little, George Daily.

B & R CAFE

Roy Hicks   A good place to eat   Phone 2531

Dick Burleson (number 37) with his senior-class teammates and the coaches of the 1956 J.B. Pennington High School (Blountsville, Alabama) football team

Graduation day, May 1957, J.B. Pennington High School (Blountsville, Alabama)

Graduation day, June 1961, Georgia Tech

Mary and Dick Burleson on their wedding day, June 16, 1961

Action shot from an early career Kentucky-Baylor game in Lexington, Kentucky

What looks like total confusion is actually officials confirming their positions on the field for the opening kickoff.

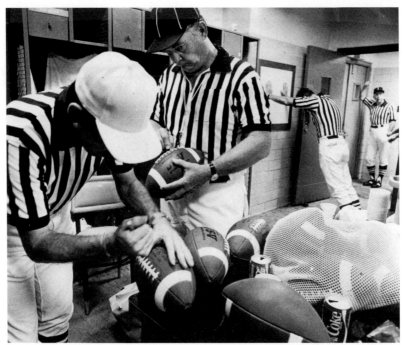

Game prep before a game at Florida Field: While other officials stretch and relax inside the locker room, Dick and close friend umpire Jim Pratt check the air pressure for the game balls.

Action shot from the 1980 LSU-Tulane game in Baton Rouge

Dick yelling to stay off the Alabama kicker. "During kicks, I found it surprisingly effective to yell, 'Stay off the kicker!' I hardly ever had to throw a flag for roughing."

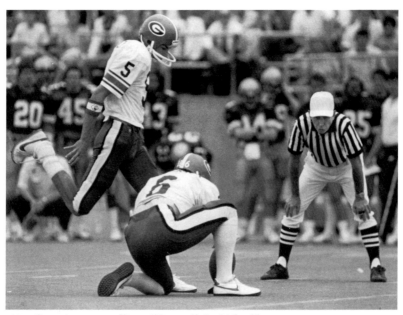

At a Georgia game yelling, "Stay off the kicker!"

Action shot from the 1982 Auburn-Nebraska game in Auburn; Mike Rozier (number 30) won the Heisman Trophy that year.

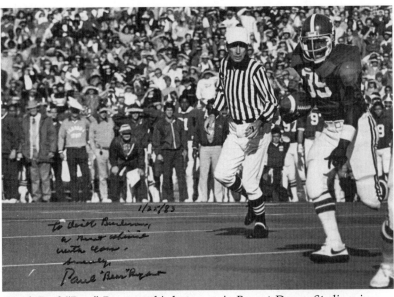

Coach Paul "Bear" Bryant at his last game in Bryant-Denny Stadium in Tuscaloosa, Alabama. According to his secretary, this was probably the last photo Coach Bryant ever signed. Dick received it in the mail the day of Coach Bryant's funeral. He wrote, "To Dick Burleson, a great official with class."

Action shot from a Tennessee game: Tennessee Fuad Reveiz's kick is good.

(From left) Ted Thomas, Ed Dudley, Dick Burleson, Joe Curtis, Jim Pratt, and Rom Gilbert with Mickey Mouse (50th anniversary tour) before the "immaculate deflection" game between Ole Miss and Mississippi State

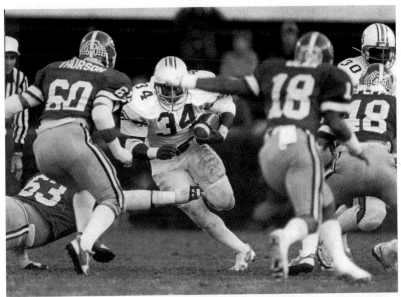

Action shot from an Auburn-Georgia game: Famous Auburn back Bo Jackson running

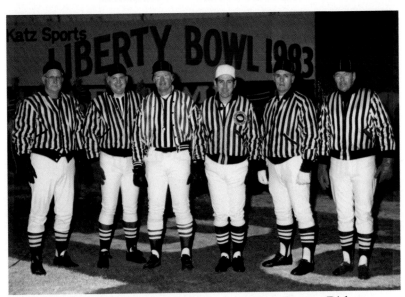

(From left) Pete Williams, Bert Ackermann, Ronnie Baynes, Dick Burleson, Ted Thomas, and Al Graning "dressed in panty hose, Vaseline, and all" for the 1983 Liberty Bowl (Notre Dame vs. Boston College) in Memphis, Tennessee; the temperature was 7 degrees Fahrenheit at kickoff.

(From left, front row) Ned Wilford, Bud Williams, John Fleming, (back row) Rom Gilbert, Bill Stanton, Dick Burleson, Harold Johnson, Billy Schroer, and Ed Dudley at the 1986 Gator Bowl (Stanford vs. Clemson) in Jacksonville, Florida

GAME NO. **3**   **GEORGIA vs. SO. CAR.**

SAT., SEPT. 28, 1985 - 1:00 PM
SANFORD STADIUM, ATHENS, GA

NO REFUND NO EXCHANGES   **$15.00** TAX INCL.
NOT RESPONSIBLE FOR LOST OR STOLEN TICKETS

This is probably one of the few times an official has been on a ticket.

(From left) Joe DeLany, Ed Dudley, Ned Wilford, Harold Johnson, Ben Oldham, Dick Burleson, and Bert Ackermann at the 1988 Cotton Bowl (Texas A&M vs. Notre Dame) in Dallas, Texas

Lining up for a kickoff during the 1988 Cotton Bowl (Texas A&M vs. Notre Dame) in Dallas, Texas; Tim Brown, the 1987 Heisman Trophy winner, is the deep receiver for Notre Dame.

The coin toss at the beginning of the Auburn-Tennessee game in Knoxville, Tennessee; Quentin Riggins, Auburn number 41, is a current Auburn football announcer.

General Dick Burleson with Senator Sam Nunn (Dick's Georgia Tech classmate) and Senator Howell Heflin

Mary and General Burleson on the reviewing stand during a Veterans' Day parade in Birmingham, Alabama

Mary and Dick at a Veterans' Day dinner in Birmingham, Alabama

(From left, front row) Dick Burleson, Butch Lambert Jr., Bobby Caldwell, (back row) Ted Thomas, Nick Buoni, Billy Schroer, and Don Shanks in front of the scoreboard at Notre Dame stadium in South Bend, Indiana, before the 1990 Notre Dame-Miami game

Ready for the 1990 Notre Dame-Miami game in South Bend, Indiana; the "Rocket" was one of Notre Dame's stars that day.

Mary and Dick on the field at Joe Robbie Stadium in Miami, Florida, just before the inaugural Blockbuster Bowl in 1990 (Penn State vs. Florida State); Dick had his right knee "scoped" a few days before, which made for an interesting ball game.

(Clockwise from left) Ben Oldham, Dick Burleson, Ned Wilford, and Ed Dudley share a rare moment of levity before they check the field for flaws prior to the 1990 Blockbuster Bowl (Penn State vs. Florida State) in Miami, Florida.

GENERAL BURLESON'S CREW
1992

Bill Bowdoin	- FJ			Charley Horton	- BJ
Tommy Lorino	- LJ	Dick Burleson	- R	Roy Waters	- U
Bobby Bernard	- SJ			James Wilson	- L

Dick Burleson's first crew under the new crew system before the 1992 Tennessee-South Carolina game in Columbia, South Carolina; note the names on the scoreboard; the movie The Program was being filmed before the game and at halftime.

Georgia's last-second loss on the last play of the 1993 Florida-Georgia game

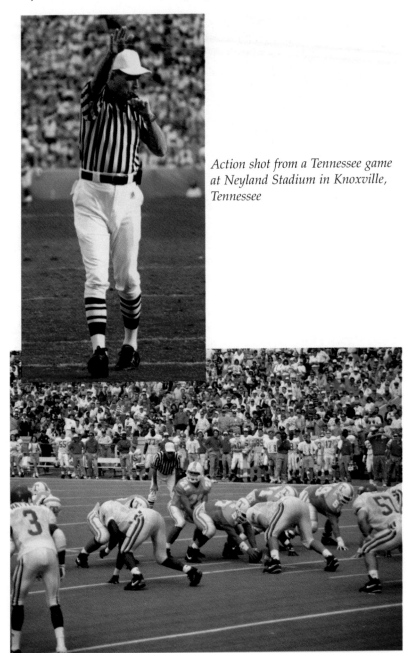

Action shot from a Tennessee game at Neyland Stadium in Knoxville, Tennessee

Field shot from the 1992 Arkansas-Tennessee game at Neyland Stadium in Knoxville, Tennessee, showing where Dick lined up at the start of a play

(From left) Bill Bowdoin, Bobby Bernard, US Navy escort, Dick Burleson, James Wilson, and Roy Waters at the 1992 Vanderbilt-Navy game in Annapolis, Maryland

Dick and Mary along with Dick's officiating crew and their wives toured the Naval Academy and had lunch with the midshipmen.

General Burleson giving a speech at the 1993 Audie Murphy Patriotism Award ceremony

Dick Burleson with his daughter Mary Jo, wife Mary, son Richard, and daughter-in-law Denice when he received the Audie Murphy Patriotism Award in 1993

To
MG
Dick
Burleson
With
Best
Wishes.
Congrats!

CJCS

General Dick Burleson with General Colin Powell; General Powell came to Birmingham in March 1993 and presented awards to several of Dick's units. Later Dick and General Powell drove to Tuscaloosa, where he spoke to the 1992 National Champion Alabama football team; they almost didn't make it since the "Blizzard of '93" was rolling into Alabama at the time.

Coach Gene Stallings ignored Dick's instructions not to give General Colin Powell "anything of value."

(From left, front row) Joe DeLany, Rom Gilbert, Dick Burleson, Ron Leatherwood, (back row) Billy Schroer, Harold Mitchell, Ben Oldham, Mike Wallace, and Butch Hannah, Dick's crew for the 1994 SEC Championship game between Alabama and Florida at the Georgia Dome in Atlanta, Georgia

Retired General Norman Schwarzkopf had 5,000 of Dick Burleson's soldiers under his command during Operation Desert Storm.

Birmingham Quarterback Club's 2000 Awards: Alabama's Shaun Alexander (Outstanding SEC Back), Alabama's Chris Samuels (Outstanding SEC Lineman), and Dick Burleson (Distinguished Service Award); this was the club's first award to an official.

Game Day—1998 Rose Bowl for the National Championship (Washington State vs. Michigan) in Pasadena, California

Dick Burleson gives Carol Burnett instructions on tossing the coin before the 1998 Rose Bowl game begins in Pasadena, California

(From left) SEC Supervisor Bobby Gaston, Bob Patrick, Eddy Powers, Stan Murray, Dick Burleson, Bud Williams, Bill Bowdoin, Rogers Redding, and James Wilson, the officiating crew for the 1998 Rose Bowl in Pasadena, California, Dick's last game

(From left) Keith Jackson, Bob Griese, and Lynn Swann, the 1998 Rose Bowl broadcast crew, visit with Dick and his officiating crew before the game begins

Action shot of the officiating crew measuring for a first down at the 1998 Rose Bowl game

Action shot from the 1998 Rose Bowl: 2nd down!

Grand Marshal Carol Burnett latches on to Dick as they walk out onto the field for the coin toss at the beginning of the 1998 Rose Bowl game; Dick sent her this photograph to autograph, but she liked it more and sent him one of hers.

Dick Burleson's induction into the Alabama High School Sports Hall of Fame in 2001

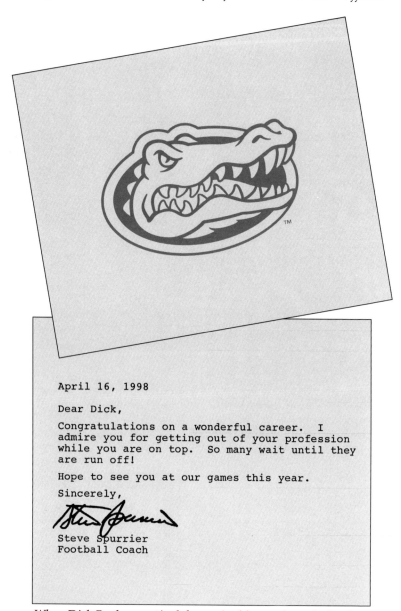

April 16, 1998

Dear Dick,

Congratulations on a wonderful career. I
admire you for getting out of your profession
while you are on top. So many wait until they
are run off!

Hope to see you at our games this year.

Sincerely,

Steve Spurrier
Football Coach

When Dick Burleson retired, he received letters from the head football coaches and athletic directors in the SEC; Dick feels this one had a message.

Dick and Mary with their family at the beach

Dick with their first grandchild, "another" Richard Burleson

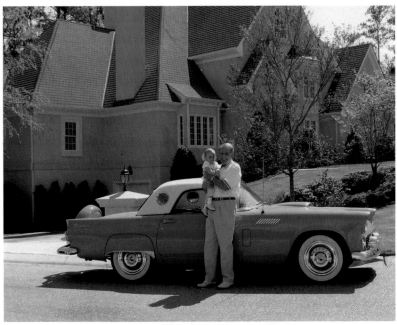

Grandson Richie trying to get the keys to Grandaddy's '56 T-Bird

Grandson Richie is looking forward to his first football game.

LSU-Tulane

When you think of bitter, vicious college football rivalries, LSU-Tulane does not immediately come to mind, but when I got into the SEC in 1972, it was one of the fiercest rivalries to be found anywhere. It was normal to have record numbers of penalties and ejections when the two teams played each other. In fact, the 1984 meeting between the two marks the only time I ever walked off the field with time left on the clock and ended a game prematurely without asking the coaches first.

It has been a great game with no fights right up until the end. LSU has a comfortable lead and adds insult to injury with a late, and some consider unnecessary, touchdown. This really makes the Tulane players mad. When they line up for the extra point, I can hear players talking to each other, explaining in detail what they plan to do to each other on the next kickoff. It is coming from both sides, and everyone seems dead serious. This is not going to be pretty.

By way of a preview, a huge fight breaks out after the extra point. One player kicks another in the helmet while he is on the ground, and a donnybrook ensues that the police have to break up. There are only a couple of minutes left on the clock, and the score differential is well beyond what Tulane could possibly overcome.

After calm is somewhat restored, I talk to the rest of my crew and explain what I think of the situation. I tell them we've already had one fight, we are setting up for another, and I don't see any way that this could work itself out to the satisfaction of anyone.

We spot the ball, and the teams line up. Before the kicker can come forward and kick however, I call it off. I blow my whistle, run 40 yards from my deep safety spot, gather my officials together, and tell both coaches the game is over. Everyone simply stands there puzzled, not sure what to do. It takes a few minutes, but finally the head coaches realize the game is really over. They come to the center of the field, shake hands, and walk off.

Florida-Florida State

There have been some seriously wild games between Florida and Florida State. I didn't work any of the wild ones. The closest I came was in 1991 when the game came down to the final seconds, with Florida knocking down a Seminole pass to end the game. I was just hoping for a non-controversial, cut-and-dried play to end the game without the officials having a say in the way it turned out, and fortunately I got my wish. One thing that was pointed out to me by my wife was that the Florida-Florida State game was the only one she had ever seen where everyone in the stands stood the whole time. She said she knew that because if she wanted to see anything during the game, she had to stand as well.

Ole Miss-Mississippi State

The Egg Bowl between Ole Miss and Mississippi State provided me with some of the most exciting games of my career, as well as the most bizarre finish I ever witnessed. The game was played in Jackson until 1991, when it began to be played on campus. It's a typical "bragging rights" game where even if both teams are bowl-bound, they focus on it as the most important game of the year. Case in point, Mississippi State went 3-8 in 2001, but one of the 3 was a 36-28 win over Ole Miss, which salvaged the season for them.

This story will be familiar to most anyone from Mississippi.

It's the end of the 1983 season, and I find myself in Jackson, Mississippi, working the "Egg Bowl" between Mississippi State and Ole Miss. It's a clear, crisp November day, with a lot of wind due to a front that had come through that morning. Memorial Stadium in Jackson has an open end on one side, and the wind has been gusting through it for most of the game. It hasn't been constant, but it has made itself a factor.

The game is nearly over, and Mississippi State is down 24-23. They have the ball and drive deep into Ole Miss territory. They run a couple of plays to waste some time and get the ball centered on the field. The clock winds down to almost nothing, and Mississippi State calls a timeout. I figure from this point they could probably score a touchdown, but they don't need one, and decide to take the more probable points.

They line up for the field goal, and I take my position alongside the kick holder to watch for any illegal hits on the kicker. This is for the game as the clock will run out during the play. The ball is lined up square in front of the goalposts; it's a short kick, and they have a very good field goal kicker. The snap is good as is the hold. The kicker kicks the ball high to avoid any would-be blockers. The ball flies straight and true, and looks like a perfect field goal.

That is, until it stops.

I have never seen anything like it. Just as the kicker's foot meets the ball, the strongest gust of the day pounds through the break in the stands. The ball begins its ascent toward the goal, reaches the highest point in its flight, and stops. The wind catches it; it spins for a second in place and falls harmlessly into the end zone.

The two officials standing under the goalposts stare at the ball for a second in disbelief. They look at each other and signal "no good"; there's nothing else they could do.

When I get back to my hotel room after the game, the phone rings. It's a guy I've known, the sports editor for the Jackson newspaper. "Dick," he says, "I know you're not supposed to talk with sportswriters after ball games, but I have a question for you."

"Okay, shoot." I say.

"We're not questioning any call, but we just about got into a fistfight in the press box over this. We're asking about a rule. What would have happened had that kick gone through and broken the plane of the goalpost but then been blown back into the end zone? We know it didn't, we got a perfect view from the press box, and you made the right call, but what if that had happened?"

"That's easy, it would have been no good," I reply.

"How does that work? I thought the goalpost was a plane, just like the goal line, and all the ball has to do is cross it."

"Actually," I say, "the way the rules are worded, the ball has to land on the other side of the goalpost or hit something on the other side of the goalpost to count."

"You've got to be kidding me."

"No, I know that for a fact. It can't just break the plane."

"Well, you better be glad it didn't do that; you guys would have had some serious trouble on your hands," he says. He is right; if that had happened, things would have gotten very ugly, very quickly.

It's amazing how strong people's memories are. Living in Alabama, I don't have cause to think of that game much, but I do speaking engagements in Mississippi quite often, and just about every time somebody asks me about that play. In fact, I was reading the newspaper on the Thursday before the 2001 Egg Bowl, and they had a write-up about the most famous Egg Bowls in history. The "immaculate deflection," as some call it, was number one.

Another interesting story about that game was that I met Mickey Mouse there. He was on a goodwill tour one year, with stops in all 50 states. One stop happened to be in Jackson during the Egg Bowl. A guy from Disney called me the week before to ask if there would be a problem with Mickey coming onto the field dressed as an official to take a publicity shot with us. I told him I didn't see any reason it would as long as he sent me a copy of the photo. He did, and it appears in this book (see page 102).

Alabama-Auburn

It may seem strange that I live in Birmingham but I never worked an Alabama-Auburn game. I was the alternate official for the game in 1975, but I never officiated the game on the field. There were several reasons behind that. The main one was mostly political. I work in Birmingham with people from all walks of life, from construction workers to elected government officials. Anyone who has spent time in Alabama knows how important football and the Alabama-Auburn game above all else is to Alabamians. My thinking was that if I were to make a call that affected the game in one way or another, it would alienate me from half the people with whom I work. I had nothing to gain and everything to lose. It was just good business sense for me to avoid the game. This was made easier by the rule that SEC officials were not allowed to work games in their hometown.

Since the Iron Bowl was played in Birmingham every year until 1989 and alternately after that, I had a perfect excuse. It wasn't until they moved it to Auburn that it became an issue. Around the time we were going to be receiving our assignments, I realized that my automatic exemption was no longer valid. I called the league office, and though I didn't officially sign out, I did make it clear that I would rather not work that game. I explained my reasoning, and they understood. They told me it was a good thing I called because it was on my schedule for that year.

I ran into Auburn Defensive Coordinator Wayne Hall at our SEC coaches and officials meeting that August. "I see you're going to be working some of our games this year," he said.

"Yeah, I am," I replied.

"I noticed you have the Alabama game."

"No, I know I don't have that one," I said.

"How do you know that?" he asked.

"Because I told them that I refuse to work that game."

He looked at me funny; he wasn't expecting me to say that. "Chicken," he said.

"Well, you can call me a chicken, but it's good for business and family—and I'd rather be a happy chicken."

Chapter 9

Great Intersectional Football Games

Intersectional games were always very interesting to me for a couple of reasons. One was the use of split crews. As I said before, we no longer use them, but it was always fun to meet those from other conferences and swap stories. One difficult thing about the split crew concept was that the coaches never quite understood when a bad call or a call that had a major effect on the outcome of the game was made against them by officials from their conference. They considered it a sort of betrayal, or at least that's how it seemed. They never really expected a break per se; they just didn't expect officials they knew to make a call against them. It's simple human nature. Fortunately the split crew idea has fallen by the wayside, and now only solid conference crews call games.

Another thing I always liked about intersectional games was the opportunity to travel to places and see stadiums I would not otherwise experience. Through intersectional games, I was able to see stadiums I had always heard about, and I found that to be tremendously enjoyable. During the split crew days, the referee was not one of the traveling officials so I didn't get to travel to a lot of unfamiliar stadiums in my early days in the league.

Alabama-Penn State

I'm working a game in State College, Pennsylvania, between Alabama and Penn State in September 1987. Both teams are among the nation's elite that year, and Alabama has several great players, one of whom is Derrick Thomas. Most people who watched him play consider Derrick Thomas among the greatest linebackers to ever play the game. One thing that makes him so great is the ferocity with which he hit people—he hits clean, and he hits hard; he would knock your head off and not think twice about it. He never resorted to dirty tricks mainly because he never needed to. He was tough, but he was a nice kid.

Sometime in the first quarter of the ball game, the Penn State quarterback takes the ball and runs a quarterback rollout around end toward his team's bench. About the time he begins to make his cut upfield, Derrick Thomas nails him. This is one of the most vicious hits I have ever seen, but true to form, it's a clean lick, nothing illegal about it. None of us think much of it—this is standard procedure. We get the ball spotted for the next play and start the play clock. The teams huddle up, and I walk over to the Penn State huddle to get ready for the next play.

I notice quickly that the players in the huddle look totally confused. I don't immediately realize what is going on, but I see that they keep looking out of the huddle toward the sideline and throwing their arms up in bewilderment. Finally, with about eight seconds on the play clock, a Penn State player walks over to me.

"We need a timeout," he says.

"Ok," I respond and call timeout; I'm still not sure why. "What's going on?" I ask him.

"We can't find our quarterback," he says.

"You don't have a quarterback?"

"We can't find him, Sir."

I look toward the Penn State side and see Coach Paterno looking up and down the sideline, trying to see if his quarterback is over there. I look around the field still not sure exactly what is going on. Finally, I see some commotion over in the Alabama secondary, and in the midst of the crimson helmets I see a single white one.

I run over to the Penn State quarterback to see what he's doing. The Alabama players are all laughing and giggling around him, and he's got a slightly spacey look on his face. "Son, are you all right?" I ask him. By this time I'm even chuckling a bit, though I'm a little worried that he's seriously hurt.

"Yes, Sir," he says, "I'm just trying to find the huddle."

The game was televised by CBS, and late in the game, announcer Brent Musburger described Derrick Thomas's performance as "the greatest individual defensive effort I have ever witnessed."

Washington State-Tennessee

In 1980 I worked a game at Neyland Stadium between Washington State and Tennessee. This game marked the one and only time I ever invoked the crowd noise rule. All stadiums in the SEC are loud, sometimes deafeningly so. When it wants to be, Neyland Stadium can be one of the loudest, if only because of the sheer number of people in attendance. At that time, Neyland Stadium held around 90,000 people. Now if you put 90,000 people of any persuasion together in an enclosed area, chances are it's going to get pretty loud. Tennessee fans are among the most rambunctious people anywhere. Put together 90,000 Tennessee fans, and you can forget about verbal communication.

The crowd noise rule is virtually ignored in the SEC. There is an unwritten law among the coaches that you don't use it. The idea is that no matter how loud a stadium gets, yours will probably be just as loud, and you don't want the other coach using it on you. It's sort of a "glass house" clause. The best example of the SEC view of the crowd noise rule came from an Auburn quarterback before a game at Neyland Stadium. I asked if they wanted me to go over the rule, and Coach Dye looked at him and asked what the best way to handle the crowd is. He smiled and said: "Put the ball in the end zone."

I'm working a game between Washington State and Tennessee, and I do my pregame coach meetings. I am required to ask the quarterback for the visiting team if he wants me to go over the crowd noise procedure. This is especially important during intersectional games since each conference has its own protocol for invoking the rule. In the SEC, for example, the quarterback (while under center) tells the referee if he has a problem with the crowd, and the referee decides if it's too loud. There is no stipulation in the NCAA rulebook for what constitutes too loud, so it's up to the individual referee to decide. Also, we found that the usual routine of having the quarterback step out from under center and signal that he can't hear didn't work because the defense is reacting on sight, and as soon as they see the quarterback move they jump. Then you get into a confusing jumble of offsides and illegal motion calls, and it just turns into a big mess.

So I ask the Washington State coach if he wants me to go over the crowd noise rule, and he assures me that they can handle the crowd. After all, he says, they have big crowds in the Pac-10, and this can't be any noisier than that. I try to convey that he doesn't quite get it, that the SEC is different from anywhere else he has played, but he will have none of it. I decide not to force the issue and let him find out for himself.

It's a close game; Tennessee would end up winning 35-23. Somewhere in the second half, Wazzou puts together a drive and is knocking on Tennessee's door. Washington State has a quarterback named Samoa Samoa who would go on to play in the NFL for a few years. Something sets off the crowd, but they get going, and the noise just snowballs. It swells and swells, and within a minute or so, it evolves into an ear-splitting roar. I can see by the look on his face that Samoa Samoa is having a hard time of it, and I know that sooner or later he's going to turn to me for help. He hasn't yet, but it's coming.

One problem I notice is that when he gets to the line, Samoa Samoa is taking his time, using long cadences before the snap. All this does is it gives the Tennessee fans a chance to get even louder before the ball is snapped to the point that nobody on the field can hear anything. At this point, the whole offense basically has to guess when the snap is coming. The tailback guesses wrong on one play, and charges toward the line. He runs the correct route—the only problem is that when he's supposed to receive the handoff from the quarterback, the ball is still on the ground. He charges into the line without the ball, catching the right tackle completely off guard and nearly causing complete chaos.

We finally get things calmed down and penalize Washington State 5 yards for illegal procedure. The crowd immediately realizes that they are directly responsible for that penalty, and they somehow manage to get even louder than before. By now my head is even starting to hurt from the cacophony, and I deal with this on a regular basis. I can feel the stadium shaking under my feet.

Finally, with a look of exasperation on his face, Samoa Samoa gives in and walks over to me. I explain the procedure with him. The way it works is that the team breaks the huddle and lines up. If they can't hear the quarterback, they go back to the huddle and try again. If they still can't hear him, I have to step in and do something about it.

On the first offense, the home team is charged a timeout, if they have any. If not, they get a 5-yard penalty. Tennessee has a timeout to spare so I take it away from them. Not surprisingly, this is an unpopular decision. The crowd doesn't get any quieter, but the yells and cheers all turn into boos. I begin to realize that we are about to make a travesty of the situation.

"Look—I have done everything I can in this situation. I have charged a timeout to Tennessee because of crowd noise, which you didn't think would be a problem to begin with. It's not going to get any better so you're going to have to find some other way to deal with it. My suggestion to you is to get to the line with a quick snap count and get the ball snapped before they can get too loud."

He follows my suggestion, but the Tennessee crowd never lets up, and the players are too shell-shocked to really get anything done. They finally give the ball up and never really recover. Tennessee wins 35-23. I am just happy to have averted disaster and gotten out alive.

Indiana University-LSU

There's a reason they call it "Death Valley." Tiger Stadium in Baton Rouge has always been one of the loudest, most intimidating places to play in the SEC. Not only has it always been one of the largest stadiums in the country, but it is always packed to capacity, and the fans are as rowdy as they come. Ever since the 1960s, it has consistently been ranked by coaches the worst place in the country for visiting teams.

It's the first game of the year, September 16, 1978; I am working a game between Indiana University and LSU at Tiger Stadium. Indiana's coach is Lee Corso, who will go on to make a name for himself in the broadcast booth. Now anyone who has watched Lee Corso on television knows how excitable and animated he is on the air. This is neither an act created for TV nor a new development in his personality. He's a nice guy, but his reputation precedes him even this early in his coaching days. He's volatile but not vicious.

This is in the days of split crews, and half of our crew for this game are Big Ten officials. My umpire and I walk into the visiting dressing room for our pregame talk with Coach Corso. The first thing he wants to know is what I plan to do about the crowd noise. This is nothing unusual—most visiting coaches of non-SEC teams want this information. I tell him the procedure, and we continue.

"Let me get this straight," says the coach. "I have to play against LSU at Tiger Stadium on Saturday night with an SEC head referee."

"That's about it," I said, we shake hands, and I leave with him standing there, shaking his head.

So the game gets under way, and as luck would have it, the first five penalties are all on Indiana—and they come fairly quickly. They also happen to come from the SEC officials. Coach Corso is extremely animated on the sideline, making his displeasure seen and heard. He wants to talk to me, but I can't go over to the sideline during the game unless there's a timeout. After a few minutes, time is called, and I walk over to his sideline to see what he wants.

"What's on your mind, Coach?" I ask him.

"Dick, I would just like to remind your SEC officials that the Civil War was over a long time ago."

"Okay, Coach, I'll relay the message," I say.

That was my only experience with Lee Corso, but to this day every time I see him, that's what immediately pops into my head.

University of Miami-Notre Dame

In the 1980s the University of Miami played a four-game series against Notre Dame, pitting one of the top traditions in all of sports against a ferocious newcomer making a name for themselves. Both teams were national championship contenders each year so the games were of the utmost importance. These were all highly charged, intense ball games, with fights occurring in nearly every game. One year they got into it at the coin toss. One year they fought in the tunnel before ever even coming out on the field. The bad blood grew each year, with both teams accusing the other of numerous improprieties, right down to the choice of officiating crews. For the final game in the series, they wanted an outside group of officials to eliminate that factor from the game.

> Imagine my surprise when I receive my schedule for the 1990 season, and on October 20 I see Miami at Notre Dame. I figure it's a joke being played on me by someone in the league office. I call the office, and the secretary answers.
>
> "Okay, you got me," I say.
>
> "I'm sorry?" she replies.
>
> "This is Dick Burleson, and I just got my schedule for the season. Some joker has listed Miami at Notre Dame on here, and I just wanted to say 'good one.' "
>
> "It's not a joke, Dick," she says.

"It's not?"

"No, Sir, it's on my schedule, too."

"So I'm taking a crew to South Bend this year? Do you realize the history behind this series?"

"Yes, Sir, that's why they chose this crew. They wanted a solid SEC crew, and the league office figured you could handle it as well as anybody."

Needless to say I am flattered at the compliment but still a little worried about the game. Fortunately they give me an outstanding crew of officials to work with; any mediocre referee should be able to handle the game with this crew. Still however there are doubts. No matter how good the officials are, they're no match for a couple hundred football players with the taste of blood in their mouths.

All the way up to South Bend, I'm thinking to myself, "I'm not gonna put up with this crap; we don't put up with it in the SEC; we have the most well-behaved players anywhere. I'm going to read the coaches the riot act before the game and put a stop to it before it begins."

At this time Dennis Erickson was in his second year as head coach for Miami, and Lou Holtz was well into his tenure at the helm of Notre Dame. I had worked with Holtz before when a previous Notre Dame team had played in the Cotton Bowl so we were familiar with each other.

Game day arrives, and it's a beautiful day—cool and crisp, absolutely perfect for football. I tell the crew about my decision to nip any extracurricular activities in the bud, and everyone agrees to it. The umpire, Butch Lambert Jr., and I go to the dressing rooms to read the riot act to the coaches.

I don't know if it's my reputation or the SEC's reputation that precedes me to the locker rooms, but some sort of discussion has taken place by the time I get there. I walk in ready for a confrontation, but Coach Holtz immediately disarms me. The minute I walk into the room, he shakes my hand and says, "Dick, we are delighted to have SEC officials here, and if you think there's going to be any hint of trouble today in this ball game, get it out of your mind now, because I assure you there will be no trouble whatsoever."

I'm not really sure how to respond to that—I am wholly unprepared for that statement. I thank him, tell him how happy we are to be there, and finish the meeting. As I'm walking to the visiting locker room, I tell Butch that it didn't work with Holtz, but I'll just give it to Erickson.

There had obviously been a meeting between the coaches because when I get to the Miami side, Erickson gives me the same speech, almost verbatim—no trouble, no problem, don't look for it, won't happen.

Still we're concerned and a little on edge, looking out for the slightest hint of animosity. One problem with Notre Dame is that the teams take the field through the same tunnel. This was the reason behind the altercation that had taken place two years before. So we have to keep a close eye on things, especially since everyone is expecting a fight. No fight comes, everyone behaves themselves during the coin toss and afterward. This shows how a coach, when he wants to, can control a team. We play the whole game, and not only are there no fights, there are no 15-yard penalties for roughness or anything, it is one of the cleanest football games I've ever worked.

An interesting side note to the game, that year Notre Dame had a great kick returner named Raghib Ismail. Universally known as "Rocket," he would go on to a stellar career in the NFL. Even at that time however, he had his own fan club. They would chant his name before kickoffs, and as I stood there beside him I'd see him smile a little bit.

So sometime in the second half, Coach Erickson has a little lead and doesn't want him breaking for a long runback, so he tells the kicker to kick it away from him. The kicker, in his desire to avoid the Rocket, kicks the ball out of bounds. At this time the only penalty for this was to move the ball 5 yards back and rekick. We respot the ball, and I see the kicker look over at Coach Erickson as if to ask what to do now; Coach Erickson shakes his head as if to say, "Don't kick it to him." So he does it again. This happens a couple more times to the tune of about 20 yards, and finally the kid is kicking from fairly deep on his side of the field. Finally, the kicker looks over at Coach Erickson, who tells him to kick it to Ismail.

He finally kicks off inbounds right to Ismail, who catches it on about the 10-yard line and proceeds to run the ball back 90 yards, practically untouched, for the game-breaking touchdown. He runs right up the sideline past Coach Erickson, who just glares at him as he flashes by.

This is my first (and only) trip to South Bend for a football game, and I soaked in as much of the experience as possible. We in the South don't think of Notre Dame and South Bend being particularly compelling or intimidating. It goes without saying that we consider our brand of football to be the best in the world, and I think that's the case everywhere. But anyone who truly loves the game of football has to hold Notre Dame and all the history that goes with it in the highest regard.

When you dress in those dressing rooms and then actually walk out on that field, there's no way to describe that feeling. It makes you think of all the legendary coaches and players who have come through that stadium over the years and how much history is in that building. And when the players run out on the field to the tune of the Notre Dame Victory March, it will get your attention.

There was an older gentleman who took care of our dressing room made sure everything was clean, that we had towels, that everything was as it should be. He was a friendly, soft-spoken man, and I can just imagine the games that he had seen, the stories he could tell. He came up to me as we were getting ready to leave after the game (this was one time we actually used the dressing room for its intended purpose) and told me he had a couple of things to say to me. "First of all, I appreciate you having prayer before the game," he said, "I don't know that I've ever seen officials do that before—if they did, I don't remember it. Secondly, I've seen hundreds of games in my life, and that was the best-officiated ball game I have ever seen, bar none."

I was touched by the sentiments; they really meant something coming from him. For years after that, he sent us a Christmas card.

Texas A&M-LSU

I worked a game between Texas A&M and LSU at Baton Rouge in 1992. The reason this game is memorable is that it was one of the most wonderful games I ever worked. From an officiating standpoint, everything went great. R.C. Slocum was the coach at A&M, and Curley Hallman was in charge of LSU. It was a close game for the most part, although the Aggies ended up winning by a little more than a touchdown.

We had a solid crew of SEC officials at that game, and since it was held at Tiger Stadium, that got the attention of Coach Slocum. He didn't make a big deal out of this, but he did mention it in our pregame meeting. I assured him things would be fine.

On Tuesday of the following week, I got a call from the secretary at the SEC league office. She told me that Coach Slocum wrote a letter to SEC Commissioner Roy Kramer. Generally when this happens, it's to complain about the officiating so I braced for the worst. Surprisingly she said he had praised us, saying that the officiating was the best he had ever seen. He wanted the commissioner to know that even though he was in one of the most hostile environments in all of college football, with a foreign crew of officials to boot, our professionalism eliminated any feelings of discomfort he may have had.

Not many head coaches take the time to write a letter unless they are unhappy about something. For Coach Slocum to go out of his way to make sure the SEC knew how pleased he was with our work not only made me extremely proud of my crew, but it also gave me a great impression of the man himself.

Army Games and Vanderbilt-Navy

As an Army General, one of the biggest thrills I ever got was working Army games. I worked Army games at Tennessee and Florida in the same year, two weeks apart. It was 1978, and I wasn't a General at the time, but I was working my way up the ladder.

Then in 1992 I got to work a Vanderbilt/Navy game in Annapolis, Maryland. The Commanding Officer of the Naval Academy invited the crew to have lunch with the midshipmen the day before the game. It was a wonderful experience; we took our families and everyone had a great time. The Admiral hosting us told me he ought to have his head examined allowing an Army General to officiate a Navy football game. Vanderbilt won the game 27-7, but it was a great game overall.

Chapter 10

Bowl Games

Bowl games are the ultimate rewards for football teams. They work year-round for the opportunity to end their season in some exotic locale like Pasadena, Miami, or Hawaii. As much of a reward as they are for teams, they are equally so for officials. To be selected to work a bowl game is one of the greatest honors a college football official can receive.

As I said before, bowl game assignments are given out by the NCAA and are assigned proportionately to the number of teams a conference has going bowling that season. The idea is that say the SEC has four teams going to bowl games, then theoretically they would have two crews of officials working bowl games. It doesn't always work exactly that way, but that's the idea. After finding out how many assignments they have received, the league office takes the officials with the highest grades at each position and sends them to the most prestigious bowl. The next-highest bowl goes to the next group of officials and so on. The only other rules are that the officiating crew has to be from a neutral conference to the two teams playing, and that if you work the SEC Championship game that counts as your bowl game.

I was fortunate to be selected to work more than a dozen bowls during my tenure as an SEC official. Not only did I have that honor, but I never worked in the same bowl twice, which was great since it meant that every time I went to a bowl game, it was a new experience. Every one of them was memorable too, either for something that happened on the field or just the experience in general.

Independence Bowl

December 11, 1982
Shreveport, Louisiana
Wisconsin 14, Kansas State 3

This was my first bowl game, and needless to say I was excited about it. There were two things I really remember from that game, apart from the simple excitement of it being my first bowl game.

The first was that I learned how Shreveport in the winter can get very cold, very quickly. The 2000 Independence Bowl was a perfect example. The weather wasn't too bad most of the day, but everything changed that night, and the game ended up being played under blizzard conditions. You couldn't even see the field. This game wasn't that bad in terms of the snow, but was still bitterly cold. It was a night game too, which made it even colder. It was brutal.

The other thing I remember from that trip was actually from the night before the game. My crew and I were having dinner in a restaurant, and there was a Kansas State fan sitting next to us. He asked us if we were in town for the game, and we said yes. He asked which team we were pulling for, and we told him neither—we were the officials for the game. He was happy to meet us and have someone to talk football with. We ended up chatting with him for most of the meal. At one point he decided to let us in on a little secret.

"Kansas State has never been to a bowl game," he said. "But I always knew we'd make it one day. Every year at the beginning of the season, I put some money in a bowl fund just in case we make it to one. And every year we don't make it. Finally this year we make it, and I'm stuck trying to find some way to spend $25,000 in one weekend in Shreveport, Louisiana."

Liberty Bowl

December 29, 1983
Memphis, Tennessee
Notre Dame 19, Boston College 18

December 1983 is remembered as one of the coldest months on record. A couple of days before we left for Memphis, the temperature went below zero. This is not unusual for parts of the country, but it is very odd for Birmingham, Alabama. The weather resulted in a memorable Liberty Bowl experience for me and my crew.

The game was between Boston College and Notre Dame and therefore was nicknamed the "Catholic Bowl" by sportswriters since both schools were predominately Catholic. Boston College had a smallish sophomore quarterback named Doug Flutie who was coming into his own that year. Notre Dame was struggling to a 7-5 record under Gerry Faust.

Game-time temperature was projected at about 7 degrees above zero Fahrenheit. Being officials in the Southeastern Conference, we weren't exactly used to being out in the cold like this. The day of the game, I called an old friend from the SEC who had since gone on to work in the NFL. I knew he had worked games in Buffalo and Green Bay and would have some tips on how to handle the cold.

"Well," he said, "here's what we do. To begin with, we layer our clothes. That's the most important part. Start with a T-shirt, then put a garbage bag with sleeves cut out over it, and follow that with another T-shirt and garbage bag. This will insulate you without being too thick. Make sure you don't put the garbage bag next to your skin as it will freeze to your skin when you start sweating. Now this may sound strange, but you need some panty hose."

"Panty hose?"

"Yes, panty hose. If not, your legs will go numb. And the last thing, and this also may sound strange, but right before you take the field, cover your face with a layer of Vaseline."

We weren't sure about all of this, but we deferred to his knowledge, and my crew of officials went to downtown Memphis to buy panty hose. Pete Williams, one of my favorite umpires, was there with us. He had played at Vanderbilt and was one of the biggest guys on the crew. We figured he would be the measuring stick by which we would figure out what size we all needed.

The wives of the crew were all there with us on the trip. After we told them what we were doing, and once they had stopped laughing, they insisted they go with us. They refused to say a word, refused to help us in any way; they just wanted to watch this happen. So with our wives by our sides, stifling laughter, we approached the counter.

"How can I help you gentlemen?" said the girl behind the counter.

I don't remember who the brave soul was that finally broached the subject. "We need panty hose," he said.

"For y'all?"

"Yes, Ma'am."

There was a pause. She regained her composure quickly though. "Well, what size do you need?" she asked us.

"What do you have?" I asked her.

She suggested the queen size for me, so I bought a pair of queen-size panty hose. Next up was Pete, who naturally asked for king size.

The wives had a ball with all of this, even to the point of refusing to help us put the panty hose on. They wanted to see if we would put it on like a pair of socks, which we all tried, before giving up and mimicking what we had seen them do countless times.

I drew the line with the Vaseline though. I did everything else, but I wasn't about to slather that stuff all over my face. That just sounded silly. However, by the time I had made it across the field for my pregame visit with the coaches, my mind was changed. I finished up my meetings and made a beeline for the dressing room and was hunting for that Vaseline. Fortunately the precautions worked out perfectly, and we were able to stand the bitter cold and officiate the game without losing any extremities in the process.

Vanessa Williams, who was Miss America that year, was a special guest of the Liberty Bowl. We got to meet her the night before the game, which was a treat as she was a delightful young lady and just a pleasure to be around. Now most of the officials' wives didn't go to the game; all but my wife, Mary, and Pat Thomas, the wife of back judge Ted Thomas, stayed in the warm, friendly confines of the hotel. Pat had talked Mary into the game as she figured if we had to be out there, they should go and suffer through it with us. By halftime they were nearly frostbitten, their feet were numb, and they were losing contact with their hands—they were miserable. So at halftime they went with Miss Williams to find our dressing room because they wanted to spend the rest of the game staying warm in there.

So we were warming up in the dressing room when a policeman knocked on the door. "There's a lady out here who says she knows you," he said, "Do you want to talk to her?"

I laughed and said, "Yeah, that's my wife—I probably ought to let her in."

So they came in, and for the rest of the game my wife and Pat Thomas sat in the dressing room with Vanessa Williams, Miss America 1983.

Another funny thing happened at that game as well. The cold front had brought with it a lot of precipitation. It had been raining, snowing, and sleeting for a couple of days. The grounds crew at the Liberty Bowl wanted to take care of the turf so they covered it with a tarp. By the time the game was supposed to start, the tarp was covered with about 3 inches of solid ice and snow. After some deliberation on how to pull this thing off, they ended up getting a bulldozer out there and just bulldozing it all off, including the tarp, snow, ice, etc. Surprisingly, this worked well. The field was a little spongy, but overall it was in good shape, at least for the first half. By halftime however, all the moisture in the soil began to freeze, and by the second half the field was like an ice rink. Receivers were sliding all over the field; nobody could get any traction whatsoever. The second half was some of the sloppiest football I've ever witnessed, but it was a lot of fun.

Bluebonnet Bowl

December 31, 1984
Houston, Texas
West Virginia 31, TCU 14

This was not only my first game inside a domed stadium—it was also my first experience with an instant replay screen. The "jumbotron," as they're called now, was strange because I found I would catch myself looking up at it to see if I had made correct calls. I had to make a conscious effort not to second-guess myself when I saw that.

The main thing I remember about the game itself was West Virginia's mascot. Their team nickname is the Mountaineers, and every time they score, he fires a musket. Of course it's filled with blanks, but it's very loud. This isn't a problem in an outdoor stadium; the sound just dissipates into the air. Inside a dome, the sound reflects right back down, making it even louder. Every time he would fire that thing, everyone inside would jump about 2 feet off the ground.

Gator Bowl

December 27, 1986
Jacksonville, Florida
Clemson 27, Stanford 21

This game was memorable, if nothing else because I got to see the Stanford band in person for the first time. At the time Clemson was coached by Danny Ford and Stanford by Jack Elway, John's father.

One thing that is unique to bowl games is the media meeting that is held the day before. It is between the television network, the coaches, the officials, a representative from the NCAA, and one from the bowl game itself. Its main purpose is to clear the air, make sure nobody has any questions about protocol or anything, and everyone is on the same page. One thing I would always bring up is that a bowl game is a neutral site with no home team, and therefore crowd noise rules do not apply.

So I bring up this point at the meeting, and Coach Elway looks at me kind of puzzled. "Let me remind you of something, Dick," he says.

"What's that, Coach?" I ask.

"Clemson is about a hundred miles away from here. Stanford is 2,000 miles away. Clemson will have 85,000 fans in this stadium, and we may have a hundred. You're telling me there is no crowd noise rule?"

I tell him that's what the book says, and he begrudgingly accepts that. Fortunately the rule never needs to be called, and everyone is happy (except possibly the Stanford fans).

Another thing I remember about that game was that they were filming one of the police academy movies at the time and used that game for some clips. One scene they did during halftime was where a guy is using a Porta-John right in front of the crowd and a crane lifts the cover off him, exposing him to 85,000 people. We figured there would be some special effect they would use to make it look real, but lo and behold they actually pulled a Porta-John off a guy while he was sitting in it, much to our amusement.

Cotton Bowl

January 1, 1988
Dallas, Texas
Texas A&M 35, Notre Dame 10

My first New Year's Day bowl game. At the time the Cotton Bowl was one of the major bowl games, and this one pitted Texas A&M, the champions of the Southwestern Conference, against perennial powerhouse Notre Dame. Notre Dame had a wide receiver named Tim Brown, who had played high-school ball in Dallas and had won the Heisman Trophy that year. It was a great "hometown boy does good" story and garnered a lot of publicity for the game, not to mention the fact that Texas A&M was practically the home team.

Dr. Pepper was a sponsor for the game and put on a lot of pregame festivities for everyone involved. The most interesting event was a barbecue for the players, coaches, and officials down in South Fork, which was where the show *Dallas* was filmed.

For the most part the game was uneventful. Texas A&M won handily, and the outcome was never really in doubt. Something interesting did happen in the fourth quarter though.

Texas A&M is one of the most tradition-rich football programs of all time. One of their main traditions is the "twelfth man." It has taken on several different forms over the years, but during Jackie Sherrill's tenure it was a program in which the kickoff coverage team was comprised of students who were chosen out of open tryouts. Surprisingly they were able to hold opponents to some of the lowest return yardage numbers in the league.

Tim Brown had a small towel his girlfriend had given him as a good-luck gift. He wore it on his belt, it had his name on it, and he had had it the whole season. Late in the game, one of the Aggie twelfth men decides he's going to make a name for himself. Brown had run a kickoff back for a few yards and been gang-tackled by several Aggie players. This Aggie player grabs the towel and ran off the field with it, waving it like a trophy. I don't really pay much attention to it, I see him waving something, but my focus is on the game at hand. Next thing I know, Tim Brown comes flying across the field after him and jumps on the A&M player's back just before he reaches the sideline.

I don't have to tell you what happens next. Both benches clear, and a full-on brawl ensues. The fighting rules were a little vague at the time, but there really wasn't much actual fighting going on just a lot of pushing and shoving. I don't know if either of the players actually even swung a punch. So since the game was almost over, we didn't bother ejecting anybody, just gave them offsetting 15-yard penalties and sent them on their way.

Tim Brown came to me after everything was over to apologize. He explained what the towel meant to him and that it was all he wanted and he got a little carried away, so to speak. I told him it was okay—I didn't know that I wouldn't have done the same thing.

I found out later that the network announcers decided that the reason we didn't throw him out of the game was because he was the Heisman winner, which ticked me off a bit since that had nothing to do with it. If we would have thrown anybody out of the game, it would have been the A&M player for instigating it.

The Texas A&M player who stole the towel became somewhat of a local hero for a short time after the game. He was interviewed on television the next day, and when he grinned, his two front teeth were missing. Through his toothless grin, he said if he'd been a little faster, Tim Brown would've never caught him.

Citrus Bowl

January 2, 1989
Orlando, Florida
Clemson 13, Oklahoma 6

This was Barry Switzer's last game as a college coach, and it was a great ball game, decided on the last play. It was exciting for me to work a game between two teams with such great traditions.

One thing I remember was that when I walked into the dressing room to talk to Danny Ford, Clemson's coach, he told me he'd like for me to meet his ball boy for the game and introduced me to Lee Greenwood. Apparently he was the honorary ball boy for Clemson, in addition to singing the national anthem. I don't know that he actually did any ball fetching, but it was great to meet him as he was a really nice fellow.

All-American Bowl

December 28, 1989
Birmingham, Alabama
Texas Tech 49, Duke 21

This was a treat for me, getting to work a bowl game in my hometown. Duke had a coach at the time named Steve Spurrier, who was working his last game there before heading off to Florida. The game wasn't particularly exciting, but we did have some excitement off the field. Our police van broke down on the escort trip back from Legion Field. Our line judge, Ed Dudley, got out of the van, climbed on the back of the lead police officers' motorcycle, and rode back to the hotel with the siren blasting. Ed was still wearing his "striped" uniform with his cap turned backward. Needless to say, he and the policeman got a lot of surprised looks.

Blockbuster Bowl

December 28, 1990
Miami, Florida
Florida State 24, Penn State 17

I had the distinction of working the inaugural Blockbuster Bowl at Joe Robbie Stadium in Miami. It was a battle of two coaching legends: Joe Paterno and Bobby Bowden. Little did we know at the time that they would end up battling it out for the title of winningest division 1A coach ever. One major thing I remember about that game was that Joe Robbie Stadium is one of the nicest stadiums I have ever been to. I have a plaque from the game, signed by both teams—it's one of my favorite souvenirs.

My story for this game had to do with my knee. I had been having problems with it for some time. Something just didn't feel right, and it had gotten worse over the course of the season. Ten days before the game, I went to see Dr. James Andrews and Dr. Larry Lemak at HealthSouth; I consider them to be the very best in their professions. They told me I needed arthroscopic surgery on the knee and that I should get it done as soon as possible. If I waited a few days, there was no chance that I could work the game. If I had the operation that day, like in the next hour or so, there was about a 50-50 chance of working the game. I chose to go ahead and get the operation done.

The problem was that my working the game was contingent on staying off the knee and letting it heal. This was next to impossible with all of the pregame activities they had. So consequently my knee started swelling, and by game time it was about twice its normal size. I could walk, but with a noticeable limp.

Before the game I had talked to Dr. Clancy, my HealthSouth surgeon. He told me he was good friends with the Florida State team doctor. Dr. Clancy instructed me to see him when I was in the FSU locker room before the game, and he would take care of me. I wasn't sure exactly what he was going to do to take care of me, but I agreed and didn't worry about it. I figured he would give me a shot to deaden it so I could stand the pain and work the game without a problem.

So I went to see Florida State's doctor during my visit with Coach Bowden. He sat me on the table and started wrapping my leg with an Ace bandage. It was already swollen, and with the bandage around it my knee looked huge. "What are you doing?" I asked him. "Are you not going to give me a shot for pain or anything?"

"Oh, no, no—you'd probably really mess it up if I did that," he said.

"Well it's hurting right now, how am I going to get through this game?"

"Don't worry, once the game starts, the adrenaline will start flowing and you won't even know you're hurt."

I told him he wasn't talking to a 19-year-old player, but it turns out he was right. My crew helped immensely. We worked things out so that I could work the game with a minimum of movement since the main thing they needed from me was my knowledge of the rules. My umpire was a guy named Nate Anderson. It's generally the job of the umpire and the referee to get the ball and spot it between plays, and he handled it for me so I didn't have to chase it after plays were over. He did a masterful job of it, and I almost never had to leave the offensive backfield. My crew was as instrumental as the doctors were in enabling me to work that game.

Another interesting thing happened during that game. Florida State has a tradition where their mascot, Chief Osceola, rides out on a horse and stabs a flaming spear into midfield. Now the NCAA rulebook states that no mascots are allowed on the field during the coin toss. I wanted to make sure of that with the coaches, so I told Coach Bowden during my pregame meeting that no mascots were allowed at the coin toss.

I have never had people come down on me like they did then and from as many angles. Florida State people were livid, bowl representatives were angry, television people—just about everyone involved was mad about that. The president of the Blockbuster Bowl told me that it had cost them $25,000 to get the horse down there. I told him the horse can run around all day long except when I go out for the coin toss. I was not a popular person with them, but I stood my ground and made sure they knew the rules.

We got through the coin toss fine, no problems. Chief Osceola and his horse stayed on the sideline, and everything was great. The first half went without a hitch. We reconvened at the center of the field for the second half for the captains to decide who is going to receive and such. I looked to the end zone, and Chief Osceola looked like he was having some trouble keeping the horse in line. The horse was literally chomping at the bit to come out onto the field. Before we got through with the selections, the horse took off. He headed just about straight toward us but off to the side enough that we knew he wasn't going to hit us. He came as close as he could get to us, chunked the spear into the field, and took off. Flags flew everywhere; we penalized Florida State, but Coach Paterno was hopping mad on his sideline. He blamed the officials for letting them run on the field; even though we had done everything in our power to stop it. Fortunately I was able to explain the situation to him and clear up the misunderstanding. It turned out to be a great game, with Florida State winning by a mere touchdown.

Copper Bowl

December 31, 1991
Tucson, Arizona
Indiana 24, Baylor 0

This was a special game to me since one of my ancestors, a great-great-grandfather I believe, actually founded Baylor University. His name was Rufus Burleson, and there's even a town in Texas named after him. I've had numerous cousins, uncles, aunts, and such attend Baylor over the years. That gave the game special meaning to me. Unfortunately Baylor didn't fare so well in the game, but it was a fun trip. Tucson is a nice city, and I wouldn't mind visiting it again.

SEC Championship

December 3, 1994
Atlanta, Georgia
Florida 24, Alabama 23

In lieu of a bowl game, my crew worked the SEC Championship in the Georgia Dome that year. This was the first SEC Championship in the Georgia Dome; the previous ones had been in Birmingham, at Legion Field. It was a spectacular game, with Florida edging the Crimson Tide by a single point. Just a great ball game all around.

One thing I do remember was that the Georgia Dome is perfectly symmetrical. There are two of everything, right down to vendors; if you see a hotdog vendor in one corner of the stadium, look to the other side and there will be another one just like him. Since it's indoors, you can't use the sun to orient yourself. This isn't a problem for anybody in the building except the referee. With everything being the same on all sides and all the switching up and moving around that is done on the field, sometimes it's hard to remember which side is the press box and which side is just a bunch of skyboxes. I can't tell you how embarrassing it would be to flip on the microphone to announce a penalty and be facing away from the press box.

One of the first things I do when I'm working in a new stadium is orient myself to where everything is. Most places have something by which you can figure out quickly which side is which, but the Georgia Dome lacks this feature. We were doing a walk-through before the game, getting the lay of the land, and I start to realize this. One of our guides noticed the puzzled look on my face and asked what I was looking for. I told her I was looking for the press box. About that time I noticed something. As you come up from floor level to the seats, there's a row of panels separating the seats from the field. I noticed that somebody had used a different color panel on the 50-yard-line on the press box side—obviously someone had noticed this problem before and had made them install the uniquely colored panel. My problem was solved.

While I'm on the subject of domed stadiums, another thing that takes getting used to at an indoor stadium is the flat field. When you play outdoors most of the time, you get used to the field being "crowned" (i.e. slightly slanted up toward the middle). This is done for drainage purposes so that when it rains, water runs off the field instead of collecting and pooling in the middle. There is no need for a crown in a dome so when you work in one, you have to get used to a perfectly flat, level field. Combine that with the artificial surface, which basically feels like a rug, and it almost feels like you're running around in a living room instead of a football field. It's a strange sensation.

The SEC Championship Game is special to SEC football officials in that it's an honor for your crew to be chosen. To be chosen for the game means that yours was the best all-around crew during the season. It's different from a bowl game; it shows a great team effort instead of an individual one. There's a lot at stake during that game, sometimes national championship implications are on the line. I had a great crew that year, and it was a terrific experience.

Orange Bowl

January 1, 1996
Miami, Florida
Florida State 31, Notre Dame 26

I was an alternate for this game. Being an alternate is an interesting experience since you have no responsibilities apart from being ready to go in if needed. You're part of the crew, but if you're not needed, you just get to watch a game. One interesting prospect is being brought in to work a position you haven't worked in years. Most alternates that are picked are referees. The theory behind this is that if the referee gets hurt, they want someone who knows the process of signaling to the press box, enforcing penalties, etc. In addition, they figure most referees have worked their way through the other positions to earn the right to be a referee and therefore can take over any other position without a problem.

As for me, I had never been anything but a referee throughout my tenure as a high-school and college official, so I was looking with some trepidation on the prospect of having to come in as another position, especially an umpire. If I had been thrust into that position, I would have been lost. Instead of the play going away from me, as I was used to, it would be coming right toward me and fast. (Nobody but an umpire wants to be an umpire. I worked a scrimmage at Tennessee one day that ran a lot longer than anticipated. Our umpire had to leave; he had a business appointment later that evening and a flight to catch. So as word got around that the umpire was going to have to leave at four o'clock, every official in our crew came individually up to me and told me exactly why he would not be able to fulfill umpire duties for that scrimmage.)

As for the game itself, it was a great game, went down to the wire, with the Seminoles emerging victorious. What I liked about that game was that I was able to enjoy it from the comfort of the sideline. It was a nice change of pace.

That covers all the bowl games for me. I may have forgotten one, but if so, it's probably best left forgotten. The last one was the 1998 Rose Bowl, and I'm saving a whole chapter for that.

·

Chapter 11

The Rose Bowl

I believe I was destined to be involved with the Rose Bowl. The New Year's Day bowl games were a huge deal in Blountsville, as I imagine they were in most small towns at that time. Every year we would go to somebody's house to watch the games, spending the whole day glued to the television. The Rose Bowl was, of course, "The Granddaddy of Them All," as the slogan states.

On January 1, 1938, the year before I was born, Alabama traveled to Pasadena to play in the Rose Bowl. My aunt was the head cheerleader for that Crimson Tide team, and that was a big deal to our family and community. She got to travel with the team to the game, which made her a local celebrity for a time.

My mother and father were also in attendance as guests of none other than Bing Crosby. I don't know for sure how the two of them became friends; my guess is that they got to know each other while Mr. Crosby was overseas doing USO tours during World War II. Nevertheless, as soon as he found out Alabama was playing in the Rose Bowl, Bing Crosby invited my dad to come to California and stay with him. My father graciously accepted the offer, and Mr. Crosby took him all over Los Angeles. The biggest thrill for my father, who was an amateur musician, was when Mr. Crosby invited him to sing a duet onstage at his nightclub.

To say that I was excited to work the Rose Bowl on January 1, 1998, would be a considerable understatement. "The Granddaddy of Them All" was the original bowl game and is still one of the most prestigious. For years it has featured the champions of the PAC-10 and the Big 10, and in 1998 that meant national championship implications. Michigan sported Heisman Trophy winner Charles Woodson and was undefeated. A win for them would mean a share of the national title. Washington State had one loss and was highly-ranked as well. This game would be one for the ages.

It was even more of an honor when I found out that this was only the second time in modern history that a Southeastern Conference crew would officiate the Rose Bowl. To be picked for such an honor was humbling, to say the least.

It had been exactly 60 years since my father, mother, and aunt had gone to the Rose Bowl with the Crimson Tide. I thought about that, and it occurred to me that this game would bring my officiating career full circle. I had been considering retirement for a while, and I realized that there would not be a more perfect time to do so. There was no way I could top this. I decided that the 1998 Rose Bowl would be my final game as a referee.

I didn't tell anyone about my decision at first. I wanted to make it a surprise for everyone, and I thought about ways to spring it on them. Finally I decided I'd just come out and say it. On the flight out there, I leaned over to my wife, Mary, and my daughter, Mary Jo, and said: "You know, I haven't told you this, but this is going to be my last game."

You could have pushed them over with a feather. After a few seconds of stunned silence, Mary Jo spoke up. "You've got to be kidding me," she said.

"Well," I said, "I've given it a lot of thought, and I've had 25 great years, and this is the best way I could imagine it ending."

Once the shock wore off they understood, and they were supportive as always. With that off my mind, the trip was great. My son and daughter-in-law couldn't make it because of a prior conflict, but having Mary and Mary Jo with me was wonderful. We were accompanied by a good friend from Birmingham by the name of Bob Patrick, who was the line judge for the game, and his wife, Emma. She and Mary played tennis together and were close, and that made the trip even more special for us.

We made a vacation of it and stayed in Pasadena for several days in order to get the full experience of the Rose Bowl. As is to be expected in southern California, the weather was beautiful the whole time, and the setting was great. I had worked more than a dozen bowl games, but the Rose Bowl is special. Not knocking the other ones, I enjoyed them all immensely, but there's just something about the Rose Bowl that no other game can offer.

We were hosted by the Rose Bowl committee, and they did a great job taking care of us. The day before the parade, they gave all the officials and our companions a behind-the-scenes look at the building and decorating of the floats and all the work that went into putting together the Tournament of Roses Parade. They followed that up with a tour of the parade route, where we could see people already lining up, camping out for the best spaces. The officials would have a pregame meeting during the actual parade, so that was the closest we were able to get to the parade itself. Our wives and other travel companions fared a little better however, as the parade committee gave them seats right in the middle of everything, where the television cameras were.

As we were touring the stadium, we ran into Keith Jackson and Bob Griese, who were the announcers for the game. This game had special personal meaning to both of them since Keith Jackson was a Washington State alumnus and Bob Griese's son Brian was the quarterback for the Michigan Wolverines. They were very gracious and took pictures with us and signed autographs and such. I told them offhandedly that it was to be my last game, and they ended up announcing that during the telecast and saying some wonderful things about me, which I greatly appreciated.

So game time rolled around, and I went through all my usual pregame activities, trying to forget that this would be my last time doing so, which was tough. I met with the coaches, got everything ready, and finally I was lined up for the coin toss.

The Grand Marshal of the parade that day was none other than Ms. Carol Burnett. As such, she was the honorary coin flipper. In my 25 years as a college-football referee, I had never allowed another person to flip the coin for me, and I wasn't about to change that. It's such a chaotic time that I tried to allow as few variables as I could. I had a specific routine: I would catch the coin, repeat the player's choice, and then show them which way was up. That's the way it worked. I had dignitaries,

VIPs, famous people of all backgrounds as honorary coin flippers, but I was the one who actually tossed it. I tried to make this clear. "Ms. Burnett," I said, "I'm a real fan of yours, I want you to know this. You're a delightful lady, and it's a great pleasure to meet you and talk to you, but I have some bad news for your coin toss. I'm going to toss the coin. A lot of crazy things can happen at the coin toss, and I have a routine that I go through to try to make sure nothing happens."

Now that was the plan. I failed to factor in that Carol Burnett is one of the most charming people I have ever met—one of the sweetest, nicest people you could ever talk to, and very persuasive. She looked at me with a hurt expression on her face. "But Dick, I've been practicing my coin toss for two weeks—you have to let me flip it," she said, and it was all over. There was nothing this Southern gentleman could do.

"Yes, Ma'am," I said. Little did I know what kind of mistake that would turn out to be.

So they handed us the official Rose Bowl coin, which was huge, and told us it's what we would be tossing. We lined up to meet at midfield. Now the way it was scripted, the referee and umpire would walk to midfield and then motion for everyone else to come out and join us.

Somewhere along the line however, things got confused, and Ms. Burnett thought that I was supposed to escort her to the center of the field. I guess she was nervous, but as I walked out from the sideline, she latched onto my arm and walked out with me. Fortunately I kept my head and didn't miss a step, and we walked out there together. By the time we were halfway out there, she had her arm around me, and when we reached midfield, she had me in a full headlock. I somehow extricated myself and motioned for everyone else to come out, including the Rose Bowl president Jack French, the Rose Bowl queen and her court, and the captains from the two teams. By the time everyone was out there, including the television crew, there were about 40 people in a big circle at the middle of the field.

I waited as they went through all the pregame ceremonies and it came time for the actual tossing of the coin. I nervously handed Ms Burnett the coin and told her just to flip it a little bit and catch it if she could. She took the coin, reared back, and flung it completely out of the circle, about 35 yards downfield. It took a good couple of minutes for people to actually find the coin and figure out which side was up. From my point of view, this was a disaster, but Ms. Burnett laughed as if it was the funniest thing she had ever seen. It could have just been nervous laughter, but she sure seemed to get a kick out of it, and that lightened the situation considerably. (Just to show you what kind of lady Carol Burnett is, I wrote the Rose Bowl committee after the game asking for a photograph of us at the coin toss, and they gave me one of us on the sideline before we walked on the field. The Rose Bowl president told me if I would send it to him, he would get Ms. Burnett to sign it. So I did, and it's in this book on page 121. Funny thing was, she liked the photo I sent better than the one she had, so she signed the one she had and sent it to me and kept the one I sent her. As I said before, she was a delight and made that whole part of the game enjoyable for me.)

We found the coin and cleared everything up, and the game got under way. It was a spectacular ball game between two great teams. Both teams had All-American caliber quarterbacks in Ryan Leaf for Washington State, and Brian Griese for Michigan. As I said before, Michigan also had Charles Woodson, the Heisman Trophy winner, playing defense. Michigan was a pretty strong favorite, but it was a tight battle the whole way through.

The game was relatively uneventful, with no strange or controversial plays, right up until the very end. I had a feeling something unusual would happen before the end of the game as my officiating career couldn't possibly end without something out of the ordinary. I was right.

Washington State has the ball late in the game, with a chance to win. The difference is 5 points, and they are in Michigan territory. A field goal is worth-less—they need a touchdown. Ryan Leaf, the Washington State quarterback, makes a first down, which stops the clock until the chains are moved. They are out of timeouts, and the ball is on the Michigan 26-yard line. There will be two seconds left when I spot the ball and start the clock. This is long enough to run another play and try to reach the end zone.

This is not long enough to spike the ball and run another play. I tried several times after the game was over to see if it was possible, and I found that even if the clock starts right when the ball is snapped, by the time it changes hands and the quarterback snaps it, two seconds have elapsed. This is not even taking into consideration the fact that there will be a delay between my signal and the clock operator actually stopping the clock.

Nevertheless, this is exactly what he tries to do. They snap it, and I'm watching the clock out of one eye. I whistle as soon as the ball touches the ground, but the clock is on zero. The game is over. Michigan has won the national championship. Case closed; it is one of the easiest calls I've ever made. Washington State wants another play, but by then I am out of there, off the field and into the tunnel.

I watched a tape of the game later, and it was touching to watch Bob Griese call the final few seconds of the game with his son leading his team to the national championship. When Washington State spiked the ball and the clock was on zero, he said, "I don't believe they're going to get another play." To which Keith Jackson, the Washington State alum, said, "I know they're not, Bob, because Dick Burleson has just left the building."

I didn't really think about that call much until I turned on ESPN that night and they were showing that play in super slow motion. They showed one frame where the ball was first touching the ground and the clock was still showing one second. They advanced it one frame, and it flashed zero. As I watched that it struck me as odd because I didn't remember it even being that close. It was a cut-and-dried call to me when I called it—something didn't seem right, but I didn't think anything else about it.

I got back to Birmingham to find a message on my machine from my friend Paul Finebaum, the sportswriter and radio host. He asked me to be on the show because a lot of people had asked him questions about the end of the game. I had been on his show numerous times so I agreed to it. I credit Paul for making me feel better about the end of the Rose Bowl game. "I've watched the replay from the end of that game over and over," he said, "and I have to admit that it does look like there's time on the clock when the ball hit the ground."

"I've seen the same thing," I said, "and it's completely different from what I saw on the field, and I really don't understand that."

"Well is the clock they're showing on the instant replay the scoreboard clock?" he asked me.

I thought for a second. "That's a good question, I never thought about that."

I went home that night, looked at the tape of the game, and saw that the clock they were showing was the television clock. The television clock is not necessarily in sync with the scoreboard clock. I've seen the television clock have to catch up to the scoreboard on numerous occasions. I realized that the two may be close in terms of seconds, but they're certainly not together when it comes to fractions of a second. I felt a lot better after I realized this; I felt my call had been validated.

The night after the game, I got a phone call in my hotel room. I wasn't there to take it so Mary Jo answered for me. It was from Dick Newman, who was the CEO of AECOM, the parent company of CTE Engineers, my present company. Their offices are in Los Angeles, and I had met him a few times. "This is Dick Newman, an acquaintance of your dad," he said. She thought it was just some officiating friend of mine, but he continued, "I just want you to know that I'm proud and honored to have someone like Dick representing our companies as one of our officers."

As he talked, Mary Jo started putting two and two together and figured out who he was. She told me about that when she relayed the message to me. I told her I hoped she had been nice to him, and she assured me that she was.

Of all the praise I received about my officiating work, this one meant a lot to me personally. My bosses, Bob Fischer and Steve Betts, had always been supportive of everything I had done in officiating, and it was great to see that it carried over to the CEO of our parent company. I also need to mention another great company supporter of my officiating— C.J. Smith, who is a special close friend and an avid University of Tennessee Volunteer.

Chapter 12

Postgame

I call this section "postgame." It reminds me of the few minutes after a game is over when you get to sit in the hotel room and reflect on things. I've told a lot of amusing anecdotes in this book, tales of funny or just plain strange things that have happened to me on and off the field. I don't want to lead you to believe that football officiating is all fun and games however. That could not be further from the truth.

Though at the very heart it is still only a game, college football, especially in the SEC, is serious business. Not only is pride a huge factor, as it always has been, with bragging rights at stake every Saturday, but a great deal of money is also up for grabs. Schools stand to make or lose unbelievable sums of money every time their players step onto the field. Between television contracts, ticket sales, sponsorships, and bowl games, college football has become an extremely lucrative business.

Because of the amount of weight riding on each game, we as officials take our jobs extremely seriously. The funny stories I have are more the exception than the rule, which is why there are so few to tell from more than 25 years in the business. It's hard to joke around with so much on the line.

Granted, funny stuff happens, but as with most things, you have to choose the right time to be funny. When a coach is chewing you out over what he perceives as a bad call, it's probably not a good time. The outcome of the game is a lot more important to him than it is to you as an official. After the game there is plenty of time to lighten up, but on the field it's usually best to try to keep a straight face.

As with any rule, there are exceptions. There are times when a little levity is admissible, even advisable, to deflate a tense situation. Here's an example.

I'm working a game between Auburn and Tennessee at Neyland Stadium in the early 1980s. Tennessee has a defensive lineman named Reggie White, whom you may have heard of. As is the norm, he is absolutely dominant, terrorizing the quarterback and wreaking havoc on the line. The poor fellow from Auburn who is in charge of trying to block him is having a terrible time trying to do so and is having to resort to holding him. Now there are different types of holding, which can mainly be broken down to blatant holding and subtle holding. A good blocker can hold a player in such a way that the officials can't see it happening and therefore don't call it.

This Auburn player is a very good holder and subsequently isn't being caught. Usually Reggie can break free and get to the quarterback or ball carrier, but it's slowing him down. He has been getting angrier and angrier by the moment, and by the third quarter he is furious. He doesn't complain for most of the game though—that's not his style. Finally he says something about it to the umpire, a friend of mine named Butch Lambert Jr. Butch says he'll watch for it, and he does. But as I said before, this Auburn player is a good holder and Butch can't catch him. A few more plays go by, and Reggie White has reached the boiling point—something is about to happen. He goes over to Butch, and starts in again.

"I'm telling you, Sir, he's . . . ," he starts to say.

Butch interrupts him. "Now wait a minute," he says, "I know what you're going to tell me he's doing. You're going to tell me he's holding you. Let me tell you something though. I've seen you play and what you're capable of doing. If I were him, I would be holding you too."

Reggie thinks about it for a second and starts to laugh, and just like that the situation is defused. Butch Lambert was one of the best at that, saying the right thing at just the right moment to calm down a tense situation. There's an art to it really.

In spite of this, I can guarantee you the most serious people on the football field are not the coaches or the players, but the officials. Officials are like the police officers of the gridiron. You have to project the image that you mean business so that you can keep control on the field. With over 200 excitable young men on the field, not to mention the coaches, keeping control of the game is the most important thing.

It's an honor to have the opportunity to officiate in the Southeastern Conference. It's an honor to be selected in the first place, and it was an honor to be able to work there for 25 years. It was a very important part of my life, one I feel privileged to have experienced.

People don't understand the relationship that officials have, especially on the SEC level. It's a fraternity of sorts, built on camaraderie and mutual respect. When we walk out on the field in front of thousands of fans and dozens of players, the men in the striped shirts are the only seven people out there who don't care who wins the game. We are the only people on our side.

It's a strange avocation, when you think about it. How many other professions involve alienating thousands of people with a simple arm motion? It may seem unrewarding as no matter who wins or loses the outcome is the same for us. As corny as it may sound, the reward for us is a job well done. If I can get through a game without any mistakes, I feel immensely proud of myself. That's the way most officials are. If an official makes a bad call, the coaches, players, and fans will get onto him about it, but nobody involved will feel worse than he himself will. Everyone else will eventually get over it, but he will never let himself live it down. I remember every single mistake I ever made.

One thing that is indispensable to any official's career, no matter what sport, is a supportive family. My son, Richard, daughter-in-law, Denice, daughter, Mary Jo, future son-in-law, Barry, and wife, Mary, have reaped the benefits of my officiating; they have enjoyed the privileges they had as the family of an official, the travel, the behind-the-scenes access at events, free tickets to ball games, and everything else. It came at a price though. As an official I had to spend large amounts of time away from home, and we frequently had to move events around in order to accommodate my schedule, or I had to adjust my schedule to accommodate them. They were always willing to work things out with me to make sure I could be there for birthdays and other occasions, and for that I'm eternally grateful. Had they not been willing to do that, I would have missed major events in my children's lives, which is something you can never get back.

Like a lot of other boys in high school in the 1950s, I didn't have time for girls—I was too focused on sports to worry about anything else. One day I got an invitation to go to a skating party. I didn't really want to go, but my classmates insisted. I couldn't skate because I had a basketball game that weekend and my coach would've killed me if I had gotten on skates. I was standing on the side, watching the people skate, and one pretty girl caught my eye. She came up to me after the party was over and asked if I could help her take her skates off. My life hasn't been the same since.

I was blessed with a wife who has been there through nearly every stage of my life. We met when I was 14 and she was 13 and have been together ever since. We basically grew up together and are as much in love today as we have ever been. We have been married 44 years, and I can't imagine a more unselfish, more supportive companion than she. I credit her for enabling me to do something I love for so long. As Auburn announcer Jim Fyffe said upon meeting her for the first time, I really outkicked my coverage when I married her.

This is an appropriate place to mention an extra bonus I received when I married Mary—a great Father-in-law (Rev. Raymond Smith) and wonderful Mother-in-law (Rachel Smith).

My career in officiating is not over now, even though my role has changed drastically. Though I am no longer on the field in a striped shirt, I couldn't very well quit cold turkey. I am still directly involved in selecting new officials, grading and critiquing current officials, and assisting with instant replay. It's still very much a part of my life, but I'm enjoying having time for other things now.

My first game out of the zebra suit was a strange experience. It was in Starkville, Mississippi, less than a year after the Rose Bowl, and as I drove there I thought to myself: "I'm not going to miss this; I'm perfectly comfortable in a coat and tie instead of a striped shirt, no problem." I met with the officials before the game and then took the elevator to the press box, still convinced I wouldn't miss being on the field. I sat down in the press box, and it was great. They had all the food I could want, anything I could need was right there waiting for me. Just before the game when everyone stood up for the playing of the "Star-Spangled Banner," I looked on the field and saw seven guys in striped shirts with their hats off. I realized I missed it. I still do, but that part of my life is past me now.

I do have to say one thing though. Officiating has ruined me as a football fan. Not to say I don't still love the game, because I do. It's just that it's very difficult for me to watch a game from a normal perspective. I was watching a game at home with Mary one afternoon, when she asked what I was doing. I was puzzled; I didn't know what she meant. She said she could see my lips move every time they lined up for a play. I thought about it, and I realized I was counting the players before the snap without even realizing it. This branches out to other things too. Whenever I see a pass go downfield, my instinct is not to watch the ball but rather to pay attention to what's going on underneath, watching for any illegal activity.

When the quarterback throws the ball, my eyes stay on him, keeping a lookout for any roughing or unnecessary roughness. I simply can't help myself.

And finally, to wrap things up, I want to say this: Not only was I lucky to have had such a great secondary career in officiating, but I was doubly lucky to have been able to hang it up as I did. As much as I missed being away from it, I felt it was time to go. Whether out of pride or love of the game, athletes and people in sports are more apt to outstay their welcome more than just about any other walk of life. After I announced my retirement, I got a letter from the head coaches and athletic directors in the Southeastern Conference congratulating me on my work and wishing me well. It was humbling, being remembered by so many of the greatest football minds out there. Steve Spurrier said it best in his letter though:

Dear Dick,

Congratulations on a wonderful career. I admire you for getting out of your profession while you are on top. So many wait until they are run off!

Hope to see you at our games this year.

Sincerely,

Coach Steve Spurrier

Afterwords

My "Closing" Story

Of all the stories I tell, this is my favorite, and I always close with it when I make speeches.

I stand in the orange-and-white checkerboard end zone, waiting for the kick that will officially begin my 1988 season. Beside me is an 18-year-old kid about to begin his college career. He looks around slowly, mesmerized by the sight of 91,000 fans, every one of them yelling for his head. It's fairly normal for a player to be intimidated by a large crowd, especially in his first road game, so I think nothing of it.

So I blow the whistle, Tennessee kicks the ball; and the game is under way. The ball sails toward us, with a thunderous wall of orange right behind it. The kid looks up, and his hands instinctively catch it, 5 yards deep in the end zone. By now the would-be tacklers are nearing the 40-yard line, and the LSU player just stares at them, slack-jawed. It quickly becomes apparent that the kid is stunned; his mind has gone blank. I can't just stand by and watch him get clobbered, so I walk up beside him and whisper through the ear hole in his helmet. "Put your knee down."

There is no response. Maybe he can't hear me. I repeat myself, louder. "Put your knee down."

This time he turns and looks at me, his unblinking stare showing no sign of comprehension. This is worse than I thought. By now we are both in imminent danger of being flattened by the incoming wave of orange. I look him dead in the eye and yell: "Put your knee down!"

His face never registers the slightest hint of understanding, but he finally responds. He throws the ball to me! I wasn't expecting this. I look at the large men about to obliterate me and the poor unfortunate soul to my left, and my instincts take over—I put my knee down.